Ron O'Brien's
Diving for Gold

Ron O'Brien, PhD
United States Olympic Diving Coach
1968, 1972, 1976, 1980, 1984, 1988

Leisure Press
Champaign, Illinois

Library of Congress Cataloging-in-Publication Data

O'Brien, Ronald F.
    [Diving for gold]
    Ron O'Brien's diving for gold / Ron O'Brien.
        p.   cm.
    Includes index.
    ISBN 0-88011-448-7 (pbk.)
    1. Diving.   I. Title   II. Title: Diving for gold.
    GV837.O17   1992
    797.2'4--dc20   91-28668
                                                                  CIP

ISBN: 0-88011-448-7

Acquisitions Editor: Brian Holding
Developmental Editor: Judy Patterson
    Wright, PhD
Assistant Editors: Elizabeth Bridgett,
    Moyra Knight, and Julie Swadener
Copyeditor: Julie Anderson
Proofreader: Jim Yeomans
Indexer: Sheila Ary
Production Director: Ernie Noa
Typesetter: Angela K. Snyder

Text Design: Keith Blomberg
Text Layout: Kimberlie Henris
    and Tara Welsch
Cover Design: Jack Davis
Cover Photo: Dave Black
Cover Model: Greg Louganis
Author Photo: George Olsen
Line Drawings: Mary Yemma Long
Charts: Kathy Boudreau-Fuoss
Printer: United Graphics

Leisure Press books are available at special discounts for bulk purchase for sales promotions, premiums, fund-raising, or educational use. Special editions or book excerpts can also be created to specification. For details, contact the Special Sales Manager at Leisure Press.

Printed in the United States of America   10 9 8 7 6 5 4

Human Kinetics
P.O. Box 5076, Champaign, IL 61825-5076
1-800-747-4457

Canada: Human Kinetics, 475 Devonshire Road, Unit 100, Windsor, ON N8Y 2L5
1-800-465-7301 (in Canada only)

Europe: Human Kinetics, P.O. Box IW14, Leeds LS16 6TR, United Kingdom
+44 (0)113-278 1708

Australia: Human Kinetics, 57A Price Avenue, Lower Mitcham, South Australia 5062
(08) 82771555

New Zealand: Human Kinetics, P.O. Box 105-231, Auckland Central
09-523-3462

This work is dedicated to my wife, Mary Jane, and my children, Anne and Tim. Their willingness to give me the freedom to pursue my career and their unselfishness in letting me help raise other people's children through sport has been truly remarkable.

CONTENTS

FOREWORD

I am so glad that my long-time friend and coach, Ron O'Brien, has finally put into book form a bit of his expertise. In my opinion, Ron is the world's best at what he does: coach diving. In my own diving career, I knew if I wanted to remain the best I had to follow the best, so when Ron received a job offer in south Florida in 1985, I followed him there from California. If I was to continue diving at the world class level, I knew Ron was the only coach for me.

Always generous with his time, Ron tried his best—and succeeded more often than not—to coach us as individuals. He understood the various demands placed on young talent, from the young kids who needed strong guidance with school, family pressures, and training to the young adults who needed a more gentle influence. Ron's knowledge of diving would fill volumes. This book is a comprehensive insight into the technical aspects of a beautiful sport.

When I was a 15-year-old at his diving camp at Point Mallard in Decatur, Alabama, Ron O'Brien was a god-like figure to me. During my college days, Ron became my mentor, and then through the World Championships, the Pan American Games, and the Olympics, he became what he remains today, a best friend.

Greg Louganis

PREFACE

This book is about diving skills, not how to train or motivate divers. It is intended to assist coaches and divers of all ability levels in understanding the skills involved in performing various types of dives and how these skills should be executed.

Throughout my career as a diving coach I have spent thousands of hours analyzing film and videotape of the world's best divers. As a result of this study, I learned that a diver must learn certain basic skills to perform all the various dives. It also was evident that although the world-class divers may look totally different in their executions because of body build, rhythm, and style, they all perform these basic skills and the dives with the same common fundamental movements. This information has become the basis of my teaching and training emphasis with all the divers I coach.

Whenever possible, I have presented the information as concepts and principles, which will result in better performance when the coach and the diver understand and apply them. In addition, the book contains two original presentations. First, the innovative technique of taking physical measurements and applying them to a formula for the forward approach will help divers of all sizes and abilities construct approaches like the champions. This system has been tested on almost 200 divers, and it works! Second, the final chapter on dive and skill progressions contains a unique series of charts that present the diving progressions divers should follow for all the most commonly used dives from the 1- and 3-meter springboards and the 5-, 7-1/2- and 10-meter platforms.

This book is organized to present the skill elements and basic fundamentals, in the order in which the coach and diver should use them. Following is a list of these skills.

1. Body alignment
2. Boardwork
3. Takeoff (balance and control)
4. Initiating rotation for basic dives
5. Basic dives in tuck, pike, and straight positions
6. Entry
7. Come-outs (slowing rotation in preparation for the entry)
8. Initiating somersault rotation and performing somersaults
9. Initiating twists
10. Stopping twists
11. All of these applied to platform diving

When you and your diver understand the fundamentals of each of these areas, and the diver can perform the correct movements as explained and illustrated, it is time to combine the skill segments into dives. The most common (and least effective) approach to learning in diving has been for the diver to perform a variety of dives first and then try to change the skill segments that are incorrect. This method puts both you and the diver in a "fix it" situation, which takes more time and is very frustrating. I strongly recommend that the diver learn the parts correctly first and then perform the dives later. To enable the diver to do this, you must organize and administer the training program so that time is set aside for work on each of these isolated skills. The diver must devote more time to skill development and less time to the dives themselves. You must measure progress by the diver's improvement in the movement patterns of each skill area, not by the degree of difficulty of dives being done.

Finally, simply understanding the explanations of the diving skills and studying the illustrations contained in this text do not complete the learning process. It is imperative that you can pick out these movement patterns and follow them when the dive is in progress, both in slow motion videotape playback and at regular speed of execution. Otherwise, you can overlook errors in performance and misguide the direction training should take. You should undertake thorough video analysis of the skills and movements during and after the study of this book. Also, you should make a videotape comparison of the correct technique and that of the diver, so you can pinpoint incorrect performance areas. Thus, I have produced an instructional video for these purposes that you may purchase (see the last page of this book).

There is little written about the sport of diving. I hope that this presentation will fulfill a need for practical, simply explained, and concise information about our highly complicated sport, for diving enthusiasts throughout the world.

Best wishes for success!

Ron O'Brien

ACKNOWLEDGMENT

My sincere thanks and deepest appreciation to all the divers I had the privilege of coaching in my career. Their cooperation with my experimentation and trial and error coaching methods made much of the information contained in this book possible. Their contribution has been invaluable.

1
CHAPTER

BODY ALIGNMENT AND STANCE

Good body alignment is the foundation of good boardwork, takeoff, execution, and entry. Body alignment involves the area from the hips to the head and the positioning of the body parts to create a straight line. When the diver achieves correct body line, he or she is not only more stable, balanced, and aesthetic but also jumps and somersaults more efficiently.

BODY ALIGNMENT

Consider that the body is a column of building blocks. Such a column is certainly more solid, stable, and balanced when the blocks are stacked in a straight line than when each block is shifted slightly off center. Also, the resistance to outside forces that could topple the column is greater when the column is in the straight-line construction, which is significant when you consider that a great many strong outside forces work to break the body parts in various directions during a dive.

When springing the diving board, the misaligned body acts as a rubber tube; it is compressible and absorbs some of the energy of the board, thus reducing lift and spin. The correctly aligned body takes on the properties of a steel rod when the board is recoiling under the diver. This is one of the unique characteristics of Greg Louganis's diving; he was the most perfectly aligned diver when jumping into the hurdle and springing from the board in takeoffs.

Figure 1.1 illustrates the typical body position for an untrained diver. The diver rotates the hips downward, causing a lower back arch. The rib cage slinks downward and backward, resulting in a rounded shape in the upper back, and as a reaction to these positions the head and neck project forward. The diver carries the center of balance back on the heels, and the overall effect is obviously poor balance and appearance.

Figure 1.1   Incorrect body line.

The diver accomplishes the correct body line by repositioning these areas of the body beginning with the hips and working upward. To experience the correct hip rotation, the diver can rotate the pelvis to an extreme downward or incorrect position (see Figure 1.2a) and then move the pelvis in the opposite direction to achieve upward rotation (see Figure 1.2b); the diver should definitely feel the difference. This upward rotation should occur to the extent that the lower back is as straight as possible but not to the extreme that a weakening or bending of the knees occurs.

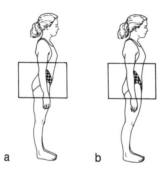

Figure 1.2   Incorrect downward hip rotation (a) and correct upward hip rotation (b).

With correct hip position as the foundation, the diver can now position the rib cage to align directly over the hips. Notice in the untrained diver (Figure 1.3a) that the center point of the shoulders is considerably in back of the center point of the hips. In aligning the upper body, the diver should bring these two points as close to a straight line as possible. In addition, as the rib cage is relocated the line of the upper back should be straight.

To accomplish these goals, the diver must elevate the rib cage upward and forward to align with the hips, as shown in Figure 1.3b.

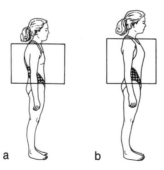

Figure 1.3   Incorrect depressed rib cage (a) and correct elevated rib cage (b).

Just bringing the hips and upper body into line, however, does not always cause the diver to achieve a straight line in the upper back. Some divers when elevating their rib cages develop a concave or hollow shape in their upper backs, whereas others develop a convex or rounded appearance.

To alleviate the problem of the hollow back, the diver must move the rib cage upward and inward (ribs toward spine); to remedy the rounded back, the diver must move the rib cage upward and outward. You can manually help the diver achieve the correct alignment by using one of two techniques to force the body into the right position.

To maneuver the diver from a concave to a straight position, place one hand on the ribs, pushing them upward and backward to keep the rib cage elevated while it moves backward. Place your other hand on the lower back, spanning the low back area to keep the hips in their upward rotated position as the ribs are moved.

To remedy a rounded back position, place one hand on the diver's abdominal area, pressing this area toward the spine. Place the palm of your other hand on the diver's low back area with your fingers spread so the thumb can press the rib cage forward to straighten the upper back, while the little finger presses down on the pelvis to keep it in the upward rotated position. The combination of these forces will help the diver find the correct body alignment.

The final area of alignment is the head and neck. The majority of divers have "forward head syndrome," which means the head and chin protrude forward (see Figure 1.4a). To correct this, the diver needs to draw the chin in toward the spine without dropping the chin below horizontal. The head should align with the rest of the body, but not to the point where it appears militarylike (see Figure 1.4b).

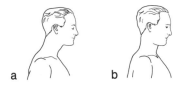

Figure 1.4 Incorrect forward head position (a) and correct head position (b).

When the diver integrates all these movements and shifts the center of balance forward over the balls of the feet, he or she will achieve the correct body alignment shown in Figure 1.5. This alignment is critical at all times during diving performance, from the walk in the approach to the entry into the water. Due to variations and restrictions imposed by different body builds, not everyone can achieve an absolute straight line, but constant training and practice can result in significant improvement for all divers.

Figure 1.5 Correct body alignment.

To maximize progress in body alignment, the diver must work to make the correct posture a part of daily life. Constantly carrying the upper body in this position not only benefits diving but is healthier than the common slouched posture most people have. You need to constantly work with the diver on these posture skills, correcting and commenting on them as part of the coaching process and giving a verbal reward when they are done properly.

TRAINING METHODS FOR BODY ALIGNMENT

1. *Using a full-length mirror.* Positioning and relocating various body segments in front of a mirror allow for immediate feedback as to what is correct and incorrect. This method also gives the diver a chance to see how much better he or she looks and reinforces continued practice.
2. *Lying on the floor.* By lying faceup on the floor and pressing the lower back toward the floor to eliminate any space in that area, the diver can practice proper alignment; because the head and upper back rest on the floor, they will automatically align correctly, enabling the diver to feel what the body line is like. You can press down on the hip and lower abdominal area to help the diver achieve a flat position.
3. *Standing against a wall.* Keeping the heels 1 inch from the wall and the head and upper back straight against it, the diver rotates the hips upward and presses the lower back as close to the wall as possible. Eliminating the space between the wall and lower back is ideal. Again, assist by pressing the diver's hips and lower abdominal area toward the wall.

STANCE

The stance a diver uses prior to the forward approach or backward press may seem simple and inconsequential, but it is very crucial to good performance and good scores. There are two reasons for this:

1. The way a diver stands and the impression this creates with the judges and spectators bear on how that diver is perceived and received even before he or she makes a move.
2. Errors in stance can be reflected in errors in the takeoff and dive.

Obviously, the body alignment just discussed is a major part of the forward and backward stance, but there are other factors.

Shoulders

The diver should keep the shoulders in a downward position, not elevated as shown in Figure 1.6a. This is important because elevated shoulders create tension in muscles of the neck and shoulder, which spreads to other muscle groups and

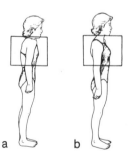

a   b

Figure 1.6 Incorrect, elevated shoulders (a) and correct, downward shoulders (b).

makes physical and mental relaxation prior to performance difficult. When most of us are under tension or stress, we have elevated shoulder positions and tension without even being aware of this. The correct downward position for shoulders is shown in Figure 1.6b.

Arms and Hands

The arms must be straight but not rigid, and each hand should be held palm in on the center of the leg, with the fingers together but relaxed in a normal partially curled position. Abnormal hand and wrist variations are unaesthetic and distracting. Keeping the hand and fingers in a rigid state causes tension to radiate up the forearm to the upper arm and shoulders, again impairing proper predive relaxation.

Hips

No twist to either side can be allowed; the diver must align the hips straight with the upper body. A torqued hip position is unattractive and can lead to an uneven forward approach, hurdle, and takeoff or to a twisted or sideward backward takeoff.

Legs and Feet

The diver should aim for straight but not stiff legs, with the feet placed evenly to keep the legs from twisting. Most accomplished divers stand with the heels together and the fronts of the feet rotated outward to create a triangular base for more stability.

Balance

The diver should maintain the center of balance over the front half of the foot. A teaching cue to determine if balance is properly placed is to ask the diver to lift the toes up while keeping the rest of the body still. If the diver does not begin to fall forward, his or her balance is not in the right place. The diver should accomplish the balance position by leaning the whole body as a unit slightly forward, not by bending at the waist.

SUMMARY

Correct body alignment and stance create a graceful and aesthetic appearance, a highly trained image, and an aura of confidence and relaxation before the dive starts. These factors add up to an overall positive impression, which can be reflected in higher scores. That extra 1/2 to 1 point more per judge on each dive adds up.

2
CHAPTER

BOARDWORK AND TAKEOFF POSITION

Proper use of the springboard is a goal all competitive divers continuously pursue no matter what their levels of skill. By the time the diver's feet leave the board on any takeoff, his or her balance, height, distance from the board, amount of somersault rotation, and in many cases the amount of twisting rotation are already determined. The importance of correct and efficient use of the springboard is monumental.

Because of the importance of boardwork, the diver must practice the movements involved until they are mastered to a high level of execution before attempting to perform them with any kind of difficult dive. Using the training methods described in this chapter, you can help your diver develop correct techniques first in slow motion and then gradually at normal speed as suggested. Then have the diver take the boardwork to the springboard and practice diligently with jumps and basic simple dives. The more difficult dives will be much easier to learn with this slow practice as a foundation.

It's futile for the diver to follow the common pattern of learning the basic motions of boardwork, learning dives, learning more difficult dives, and then trying to correct and improve boardwork at a later date. Many bad habits learned in the beginning because of lack of patience, practice, and attention to detail become ingrained and uncorrectable and remain throughout the diver's career.

Practice doesn't make perfect; perfect practice makes perfect!

THE FORWARD APPROACH

Now that the diver is standing in a straight line, with no twists or unevenness in body segments and with the balance slightly forward, work on the forward approach can begin. The overall effect of the approach should be a smooth, even flow of motion. No one part of the movement pattern should stand out. At the same time, the diver needs to attain excellent height and balance in the hurdle and takeoff. You can achieve this by following certain guidelines in constructing the approach.

1. Utilizing a moderate rate of speed in the steps
2. Determining the length of the steps and hurdle relative to the diver's size
3. Eliminating unnecessary movements by establishing a consistent timing pattern between the arms and legs
4. Applying force within the boundaries of smoothness

For each part of the approach, the diver should adhere to these guidelines. The result will be an appealing, efficient, effective blend of motion. The forward approach is illustrated in Figure 2.1, a-q. Refer to this figure as each segment of the approach is described in the following sections.

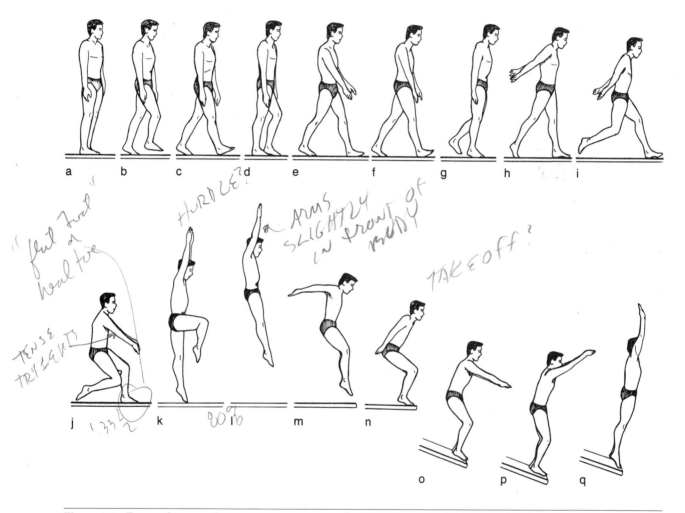

Figure 2.1   Forward approach.

Number and Speed of Steps

The diver can use 3, 4, or 5 steps in the approach. The 4- or 5-step approach is recommended because it gives the diver more time to establish a good rhythm before taking the faster and stronger step prior to the hurdle. Divers using the 3-step approach tend to walk too fast and rush the hurdle.

Two factors will dictate the number of steps taken.

1. Which leg the diver uses to begin the approach
2. Which leg the diver uses to lift into the hurdle

If the diver uses the same leg for the 1st step as is lifted into the hurdle (the hurdle leg), then a 4-step approach must be used. If the diver uses one leg to start the approach and the other as the hurdle leg, then a 3- or 5-step approach must be used. The reason for this is simple: When the same leg is utilized for both the 1st step and the hurdle, the hurdle can occur only after the 2nd or 4th steps; when opposite legs are employed for the 1st step and the hurdle, the hurdle can occur only after the 3rd and 5th steps. Therefore, diver preference based on what feels best with regard to the starting leg and hurdle leg determines the number of steps to be taken.

The speed of the steps needs to be moderate, so the diver appears to be neither rushed nor lacking in continuity. Experimentation with various speeds has shown that a speed of 75 to 90 beats per minute, depending on the size of the diver, best accomplishes this result. By having the diver perform the approach using a metronome set to varying speeds, you can determine a "best" speed for each individual. Obviously, 75 to 90 beats per minute is a target area you should use as a starting point. Each diver will have his or her own comfortable rhythm; however, if this rhythm is 50 or 120 beats per minute, the net effect is probably not going to be good.

Constructing the Approach

When diver or coach is left to design a forward approach with few or no parameters, the results are extremely diverse, sometimes even humorous. By using certain physical measurements and applying them to a formula, you can develop a very specific approach. With this as a beginning point, you and the diver can then adopt changes to meet individual needs.

You need two diver measurements to begin constructing the approach.

1. Distance in inches from the top of the fibula (side of the lower leg) to the ground
2. Length of the foot in inches

Measuring foot length is no problem; however, you must be able to find the top of the fibula to complete the measurements. The fibula is located on the side of the knee at the approximate level of the bottom of the knee cap. Have the diver stand with the leg to be measured slightly bent. By probing this area you will find a space between the bone of the upper leg (femur) and that of the lower leg (fibula). Locate the top of the fibula, and then have the diver straighten the leg. Measure the distance from this point to the ground. (The diver must not be wearing shoes.)

Add these two numbers together to determine the basic step length of the approach. Then establish the size of the steps and hurdle as follows:

Hurdle = 80 percent of the step length, to the nearest 1/2 inch

Example: Length from midknee to ground = 17-1/2 inches
            Length of foot = 9-1/2 inches
                  Total = 27 inches

80 percent of 27 inches = 21.6 inches to nearest 1/2 inch = 21-1/2 inches

Last step (step prior to hurdle) = step length + 33-1/3 percent

Example: Step length = 27 inches
            Last step = 27 inches + 9 inches = 36 inches

Intermediate steps = step length (in this case 27 inches) *30"*

These steps consist of 1 step for a 3-step approach, up to 3 steps for a 5-step approach.

First step = 90 percent of step length, to nearest 1/2 inch *27"*

Example: Step length = 27 inches

90% of 27 inches = 24.3 inches to nearest 1/2 inch = 24-1/2 inches

When marking off this approach on a board or on the ground, begin from the tip of the board and work back to the starting point. After the diver practices with this for a reasonable time, determine whether he or she has great difficulty performing a good approach, and make adjustments as necessary to fit the diver's needs.

The basic principle here is that the approach is a function of a basic unit (step length) with adjustments in various areas for specific reasons. The diver should take the 1st step with less leg swing than the intermediate steps, because the diver initiates the step with the legs together rather than swinging them from a position behind the body; thus we calculate the 1st step as 90 percent of step length. The last step prior to the hurdle is performed as a faster, stronger step than the intermediate steps; therefore, we calculate 33-1/3 percent longer length to accommodate this. If this 33-1/3-percent longer step does not work well, then measure the diver's standing height and use 60 percent of this figure as the length of the last step. Observation and experimentation with various-sized divers show that the 80 percent of step length recommendation for the hurdle allows the hurdle length to provide sufficient horizontal velocity to the end of the board, but does not make the hurdle so long that getting to the tip of the board is difficult for the diver. The 80 percent value also means the diver takes the hurdle from a more springy area of the board, resulting in more height. Figure 2.2 illustrates this formula mapped out on a diving board.

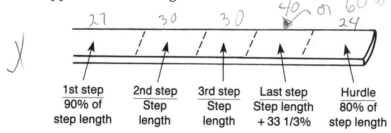

Figure 2.2   Approach formula mapped out on a diving board.

Placement of the Foot on the Board

During the steps prior to the hurdle, the foot should strike the board in the normal heel-to-toe walking action. As the diver goes into the hurdle, he or she should either use a heel–toe placement of the foot or should place the whole surface of the foot on the board simultaneously. These two methods more effectively allow the diver to transfer body weight over the pushing leg into the hurdle, and therefore these methods provide a better balance. Placing the foot down with the ball of the foot first impedes the body weight moving forward and tends to create a backward lean in the hurdle. Most top divers use the method of placing the whole foot simultaneously on the board going into the hurdle.

Arm Swing and Timing With Steps

Using arm swing in the approach is important for the diver to achieve rhythm and timing as well as to increase the amount of lift into the hurdle. By developing a simple but concise timing of the arm swing with the steps in the approach, the diver can establish a pattern of movement that is consistently repeated.

Other than the use of the arms in the walk, there is no difference between the 3-, 4-, or 5-step approach. In the 3-step approach the arms swing forward on the 1st step, in the 4-step approach they swing forward on the 2nd step, and in the 5-step approach they swing forward on the 3rd step. The key factor in all the approaches is the point at which the arms begin to swing forward in relation to the leg action. The diver can adapt the basic timing principle from the 4-step method described here.

In the 4-step approach, the arms hang naturally at the sides during the 1st step. The instant the heel contacts the board in the 2nd step the forward arm swing begins, ending at a point 1 to 1-1/2 feet in front of the body, depending on the diver's preference. When the heel contacts the board in the 3rd step, a backward arm swing begins, ending 1-1/2 to 2 feet behind the body. The diver should finish this backward swing with the arms starting the final forward swing into the hurdle, just before the foot is placed on the board in the 4th step.

The critical timing factor here is that the diver start the forward and backward arm swings the instant after the foot contacts the board in the 2nd and 3rd steps. If the arm swings are too early the arms either will have to hesitate, thus ruining the rhythm and flow of motion, or will be too early into the hurdle, causing poor height and balance. Should the arms start late, they will not be behind the body and ready to start the hurdle at the right time, which results in a very fast backward–forward motion of the arms during the 4th step. Again the rhythm and flow are disrupted and poor balance (usually a backward lean) occurs in the hurdle.

Throughout the arm swing movements, the diver should relax the muscles in the arms and hands with the exception of the triceps, which is the muscle located on the back of the upper arm. The triceps, when maintained in a contracted state, keeps the elbow extended so no arm bending can occur. This is most important during the forward swing of the arms into the 4th step in preparation for the hurdle, and during the hurdle, press, and takeoff. The diver should not, however, contract the triceps maximally so a stiff appearance occurs but instead should contract the muscle just enough to keep the arms straight.

Balance

Throughout the steps of the approach, the diver should keep the body weight forward over the front part of the foot (an alignment described in chapter 1). This is especially important during the 2 steps prior to the hurdle. If the diver holds the arms in a backward position while stretching out for the longer last step, this will create a strong tendency for the balance to fall backward. The diver must counteract this by keeping a definite forward lean of the body through this portion of the approach.

The Hurdle and Press

As the diver places the foot on the board after the last step, the knee and hip joints of that leg (the ''drive'' leg) flex and the body weight drops while the arms begin their swing forward and up; then the other leg (the hurdle leg) starts its forward and upward lift.

The diver should keep the arms straight and parallel, with the wrist, elbow, and shoulder joints in a neutral, natural position. No unusual rotation of these joints in the inward or outward direction should occur. As the arms and hurdle leg approach their final positions for takeoff into the hurdle, the drive leg extends to a straight line at the hip, knee, and ankle joints, propelling the body upward. For the takeoff position for the hurdle, the diver holds the arms straight, parallel, and located overhead slightly in front of the body; the head should be in a neutral position with chin drawn in so the diver can see the tip of the board. The hurdle knee should be positioned with the thigh horizontal and the lower leg vertical, causing a 90-degree angle in the knee joint, and with the ankle and foot of the hurdle leg pointed. The diver should be able to sight down the inside of the lower leg and foot to the tip of the board when the hurdle leg is lifted; this will help the diver make sure the position is correct. Study this position in Figure 2.3; it is critical to a balanced and controlled hurdle and takeoff.

Figure 2.3   Hurdle takeoff position.

As the body rises from the board, the knee of the hurdle leg begins a smooth and gradual extension so the legs are together with toes pointed at the peak of the hurdle, while the arms remain in the hurdle takeoff position. The diver must lift the knee into the hurdle and extend the knee without any hesitation or detectable change in speed. If a jerky high-speed drop of the hurdle leg occurs while the body is in the air, a backward movement of the torso will occur.

When the body starts its descent from the top of the hurdle to the board, the arms begin to swing backward and downward.* The diver must time this arm swing so the arms pass the hips as the feet land on the board. If the diver keeps the arms straight, the hands will pass the legs at approximately the level of the knee joint.

Just before the diver contacts the board, the hips and knees flex and the toes are drawn up so the landing occurs on the balls of the feet, hip-width apart. As the body weight drops onto the board, the heels will come down to make contact with the board. While the arms continue their path past the legs and up to the overhead takeoff position, the body extends and the recoil of the board propels the diver into the air. The diver must bring the feet and legs back together tightly as he or she leaves the board.

Visual Focus

Throughout the approach, the diver should focus the eyes on the tip of the board, which is the target; the diver must focus concentration on this target to ensure the best chance to hit the mark. Just prior to landing on the board, the diver should shift the focus of the eyes to the far side of the pool in front while the head lifts

---

*Depending on the height of the hurdle, the quickness of the diver, and the diver's arm length, this motion may start somewhat later, but if it is delayed very long, the arms will be late getting into the position for the takeoff.

slightly to a neutral position for the landing. *The diver must not watch the feet make contact with the board.*

TRAINING METHODS FOR THE FORWARD APPROACH

1. *Floor work.* Have the diver accurately measure his or her approach on the floor, marking with tape the points at which each step should occur and the point where the hurdle should land on the tip of the board.

   The diver should then slowly walk through the movements of the steps, hurdle, and front jump, stopping after each step to check balance, body alignment, and position of arms. After performing the 4th step and lifting the arms and leg into the hurdle motion, the diver should stop and hold the correct hurdle position while balancing on the toes of the drive leg. By learning to perform the perfect hurdle takeoff position in this way, a diver greatly increases his or her chance of transferring this position to an actual approach on the springboard. After balancing in the hurdle takeoff position for 2 to 3 seconds, the diver should place the toes of the hurdle leg on the mark indicating the end of the board and bring the legs together while holding the arms still. This simulates the drop of the knee that occurs while the body is rising to the top of the hurdle. Next the diver swings the arms backward and downward as the body crouches into the springing position so the arms are beside the hips at the end of the downward movement. The arms continue upward in front of the body and to a position 45 degrees above horizontal, then the diver performs a front jump with an overhead reach of the arms.

   As the diver's movements and positions become more accurate, increase the speed of the practice gradually. However, continue to have the diver practice holding the hurdle takeoff position for 2 to 3 seconds before he or she continues the press and takeoff. When the diver can balance the hurdle takeoff position consistently and in the proper position, instruct him or her to practice the walk-through with a jump into the hurdle; the diver should swing the arms down from the hurdle so they pass the hips while the diver lands.

2. *Mirror work.* Have the diver perform the same drill in front of a full-length mirror. The diver can practice the hurdle takeoff, holding for 2 to 3 seconds from both a front and a side view, so he or she can monitor all aspects of the correct position.

   I cannot overemphasize the importance of extensive, continuous practice of the approach at slow then faster speeds on the floor and in front of the mirror. Great patience and perfectionism here can ensure a great forward approach, hurdle, and takeoff.

3. *Metronome.* A metronome set to the desired speed of the approach can help the diver tremendously in developing a consistent rhythm of steps and hurdle. The diver can use this not only for floor and mirror work but during actual diving practice. For most divers, 75 to 90 beats per minute works well as a target speed.

4. *Length of last step.* Most divers tend to make the last step of the approach too long and the hurdle too short. To help the diver learn to correct this problem, tie a 4-foot length of surgical tubing around the board at the point where the 4th step should end, and then have the diver practice both on the dry-land board and in the pool with the tubing in place. Each time the diver oversteps the mark, contact with the tubing will instantly tell him or her that the 4th step was too long. This also gives the diver a visual cue as to where to place the foot correctly. Eventually, the tubing will no longer be needed, but whenever the problem recurs you should put the rubber tubing back on the board. If the

diver takes too short a last step, place the rubber tubing in a position that forces the diver to step over the tubing and thus take a longer last step.

5. **Knee extension timing.** The knee action of the hurdle leg should be continuous and smooth so that there is no stop of the hurdle leg in the lifted position. As soon as the leg reaches its proper position at the point of takeoff for the hurdle, it should immediately begin to extend as the body rises to the top of the hurdle. To emphasize and learn this motion, the diver should practice taking the 4th step of the approach and the hurdle from the ground or deck onto a bench or stair step, landing with the arms overhead and the legs straight and feet together. Adjust the height of the landing platform to the strength of the diver so the diver is just able to get the feet together prior to landing. If this preferred height is not possible, any bench or step height is better than none.

6. **Arm timing.** A common tendency is for a diver to hold the arms in position too long at the top of the hurdle, thus making it impossible to get the arms down, past the hips, and back overhead in time for the takeoff. To alleviate this error, have the diver practice stepping off a platform or step with the arms in the position desired at the top of the hurdle. As soon as the body begins dropping to the landing spot, the diver should begin to circle the arms backward and downward. The diver should land on the toes, with feet close together and the shock of landing absorbed in the knees and hips. The arms should be timed so they are just beside the hips at the point of contact with the ground.

COMMON FORWARD APPROACH
MISTAKES AND CORRECTIONS

Mistake	Correction
The diver approaches too fast.	Roll the fulcrum back several inches beyond the normal setting. As you see the speed slowing down to accommodate the slower board movement, place the fulcrum back to the original position. Repeat the process until a change occurs. Have the diver practice the approach in time with a metronome set to the desired speed.
The diver places the foot down toes first going into the hurdle.	Instruct the diver to place the heel down first. This makes it much easier for the diver to feel this major change than if you instruct him or her to place the whole foot at one time.
The diver bends the elbows excessively in the hurdle and press.	Find or make elbow braces that prohibit arm bending, and instruct the diver to practice approaches while wearing the braces.

Mistake	Correction
The diver hurdles too long or short.	If using rubber tubing doesn't work, adjust the diver's approach length. Divers who have practiced the approach for a year or more may find it almost impossible to change the length of the last step to adjust hurdle length. Therefore, if the hurdle is too short, lengthen the approach by the distance you wish to lengthen the hurdle, and vice versa for a hurdle that is too long.
The diver swings his or her arms down too early from the hurdle (typical of young divers and gymnasts).	Make the diver touch the sides of the knees with the fingertips when landing on the board. This cannot be done when the arms swing too early.
The diver swings the arms down too late from the hurdle.	Same method as for early arm swing.
The diver constantly over-jumps the end of the board.	If the diver is using correct hurdle technique, lengthen the approach. If this doesn't work, make the diver walk more slowly.
The diver lands short of the tip of the board.	If the diver is using correct hurdle technique, shorten the approach by the distance the diver misses the end of the board. Making the diver walk slightly faster can also help.
The diver constantly misses the timing of the board on takeoff.	This is caused when the diver swings the arms and lifts the knee too fast into the hurdle. It occurs frequently during difficult optional dives and in competition. Tell the diver to take a longer backswing of the arms in the next-to-last step, which will cause the diver to take more time to complete the movements. If this doesn't work, roll the fulcrum forward slightly.

BACKWARD PRESS

The backward press is much less complicated and demanding than the forward approach. For this reason it very often doesn't command as much attention and practice as it should. Depending on dive selection, 40 to 50 percent of all dives in the competitor's program begin with the backward press, so effective performance of it is extremely important.

Even though there are almost as many variations of this skill as there are divers performing it, only two methods are included here. The first is recommended for beginners and beginning competitive divers because of its simplicity. Once the diver attains a suitable level of balance and skill, you should teach the second and more complicated backward press.

Proper body alignment and stance, as mentioned in chapter 1, are paramount to successful performance of the backward press; the diver must possess all the elements of proper alignment and stance before starting the first motion.

2-Part Backward Press (Beginning Divers)

The diver stands with the heels slightly above horizontal. The 2 parts of this press are described below and illustrated in Figure 2.4, a-g.

Part number	Description
1	The arms and ankles begin moving simultaneously in an upward direction. As the arms lift laterally to a position 45 degrees above horizontal and slightly in front of the body line, the diver lifts the heels to their highest position. This is called the top of the press.
2	The arms circle down and back as the body flexes at the hips and knees and the body weight begins to drop. At the end of this squatting movement, the diver keeps the heels slightly above a horizontal position as the arms pass the hips and begin their upward swing in front of the body; the diver keeps the arms parallel and as straight as possible. After the upswing of the arms, the body begins to extend and the board recoils to propel the diver upward.

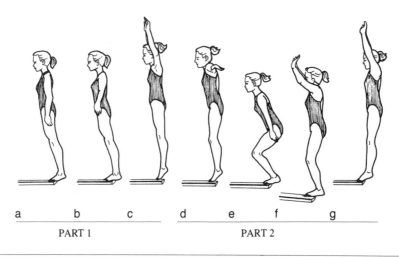

a   b   c   d   e   f   g

PART 1   PART 2

Figure 2.4   2-part backward press.

4-Part Backward Press

The starting position for this press is the same as for the 2-part press; the heels are just above horizontal. The 4 parts of this technique are described here and shown in Figure 2.5, a-j.

Part number	Description
1	Without any other motions, the diver lifts the heels to their highest point.
2	The diver brings the heels down to the original starting position while lifting the arms laterally and slightly in front of the body line, to shoulder level. (This is called opposition, because the heels and arms move in opposite directions.)
3	As the arms continue to move upward to a position 45 degrees above horizontal and slightly in front of the body, the heels again rise to their highest point. The tops of the press positions in the 2-part press and the 4-part press are identical.
4	The arms circle back and down as the body crouches into the springing position. This follows the same sequence of movement as the 2-part press.

Note: The speed of the ankle movement dictates the speed of the arm motions in Parts 2 and 3. Because a quick movement of the arms is not desired, it is important for the diver to keep the ankle motions moderate in speed.

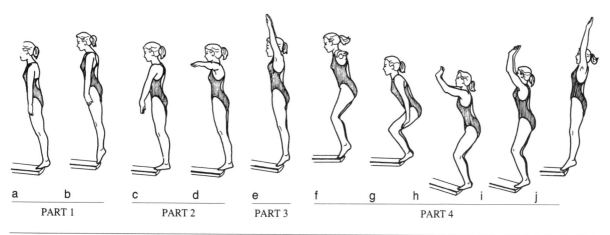

a   b   c   d   e   f   g   h   i   j

PART 1   PART 2   PART 3   PART 4

Figure 2.5 4-part backward press.

The 2-part press is simple and is relatively easy for the beginner to learn while he or she is still grappling with maintaining balance and distance from the board. To introduce the 4-part press at this point would tremendously complicate the situation. However, even though the 2-part press is simple, it causes the diver to move too quickly in springing the board and to apply too much force in Part 1 and too little force in Part 2. For these reasons, you should teach the 4-part press as soon as you feel the diver can accomplish it.

Why The 4-Part Press?

There are some specific reasons for a diver to use this press; it allows consistent balance and good resulting lift from the springboard.

During this press the diver's heels lift initially in an upward motion because this helps keep body weight over the front of the foot, where the toes can create pressure on the board to adjust balance and control. A downward ankle motion as the starting movement tends to drop the body balance backward.

By using opposition of arm and ankle actions in Part 2, the diver achieves slower arm motion because the arms must wait for the heels to go down and then back up as the arms lift to an overhead position at the top of the press. When the arms and heels lift simultaneously, this generally creates a much faster movement, making balance more difficult. Also, by keeping the arms slightly in front of the body line at this time, the diver keeps balanced on the board while the heels drop and the board moves downward (both motions can cause the diver to fall backward).

By analyzing frame by frame the execution of various methods of backward press, we can see that no matter how many board rocks a diver takes or how much speed and force the diver applies in the movements to the top of the press, when the top of the press is achieved the springboard is level and motionless. No energy is stored in the board; thus, the concept that harder and more oscillations of the board will cause it to rise higher prior to the press is incorrect. Therefore, all movements the diver makes in reaching the top of the press serve to establish a rhythm and balance as well as to elevate and stretch the body in preparation for the dropping of the body weight and acceleration of the arms into the press.

Thus, excessive rocking of the board does not result in more spring and merely increases the diver's chance of losing balance. More forceful upward movements of the arms and body also make balance more difficult and are a waste of energy.

Visual Focus

The most important factor here is not so much the point on which the diver focuses but rather the position of the head, which should be held erect and in line through the backward press. However, the point of focus does play a part: If the diver focuses on a point somewhere between the fulcrum and the back of the board, the correct head position is easier to achieve than if the diver looks down at a point more forward on the board.

Arms and Hands

Throughout the press, the diver should keep the hands in a neutral and natural position, with no inward or outward rotation of the palms or shoulder joints. As the arms circle back and down from the top of the press, the diver's quickness and shoulder flexibility dictate the distance behind the body that the arms travel. If the diver swings the arms back to the point where the shoulders and upper body are pulled backward, an off-balance takeoff will result. Also, the farther back the arms circle, the more difficulty the diver will have getting them to the overhead takeoff position at the proper time.

Throughout the lifting and swinging motions, the diver should keep the arms straight, using the triceps muscles. During the upward swing of the arms prior to takeoff, most divers do bend the elbows somewhat to accelerate this motion, allowing the arms to reach the necessary takeoff position in time. However, keeping the arms straight at this point is desirable if done with proper speed and timing.

Foot and Ankle Position

The diver should keep one third to one half of the feet's surfaces on the board to aid in balance and to prevent slipping. The diver should keep the heels slightly elevated to compensate for the downward angle of the board from the diver's weight. Standing very high on the toes is an unstable and difficult balancing position. At no time during the backward press should the heels drop below the board level. For lateral balance and good jumping position, the diver should use a triangular placement of the feet with the heels together and the fronts of the feet about 2 inches apart.

TRAINING METHODS FOR THE BACKWARD PRESS

1. *Floor work.* Have the diver slowly go through the movements of the backward press; both of you should pay attention to detail and be sure that each action is correct. As the motions become more natural and consistent, have the diver gradually increase the speed until the diver is performing the motions at the speed to be used on the springboard. Then instruct the diver to practice the backward press with a jump. As the diver's arms pass the legs at the bottom of the press, the arms should continue to swing upward in front of the body to a position 45 degrees above horizontal. Then the diver should initiate the backward jump with the legs as the arms move to an overhead reaching position.

2. *Mirror work.* Using a full-length mirror, the diver should go through the backward press motions in the same manner as described in the previous training method. Have the diver perform the actions both from a forward and side view.

3. *Bench work.* Have the diver stand on a low bench or step and use the same practice pattern used in the previous two training methods. This allows the diver to achieve accuracy of movement and balance with the foot in the same position as when on the springboard.

4. *Side of pool.* Have the diver perform the press at the same speed as on the springboard and do a backward jump.

TAKEOFF POSITION

One basic preliminary takeoff position of the body and arms is common to all takeoffs regardless of direction of rotation or the number of somersaults or twists to be performed. The diver flexes the knees and hips and initiates a jumping movement while holding the arms above and in front of the body. This position is illustrated in Figure 2.6, a and b, for the forward approach and backward press takeoffs. Note that they are identical, except for the direction the diver is facing.

This preliminary takeoff position occurs just before the springboard begins its recoil. What happens after this point is determined by the dive to be performed. These body motions, positions, and balances will be described later as the dives are explained.

Figure 2.6 Preliminary takeoff position for the forward approach (a) and backward press (b).

The most important concept is that not only are the arms above and in front of the body before the board propels the diver upward, but the arms are also in this position before the diver fully extends the legs in the jumping action. This arm timing in relation to the movement of the legs causes most divers trouble in take-offs. In the vast majority of cases, the diver's arms are late getting to this position and therefore cannot assist correctly in the remaining part of the takeoff.

This arm timing is so difficult to achieve because it is an unnatural jumping motion, contrary to all the basic jumping activities we learn as children. When we jump to grab a bar overhead or to catch a ball, the arms and legs move simultaneously. This is illustrated in Figure 2.7, a-d; in a normal jump, the arms swing upward as the legs extend to thrust the body into the air. In contrast, during all diving takeoffs the arms swing upward before the legs extend to begin the jump (see Figure 2.8, a-d).

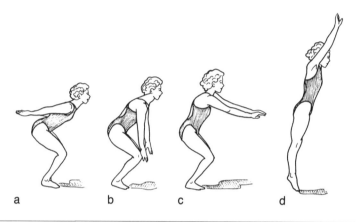

Figure 2.7   Normal jump.

Figure 2.8   Diving jump.

This difference is extremely important for the diver to understand as early in training as possible. Practice for this arm timing is incorporated into the floor work exercises described under Training Methods for the Forward Approach and Backward Press earlier in this chapter. It's critical that the diver practice this correct but unnatural jumping action at all times during dry-land boardwork drills and while doing forward and backward jumps from the springboard.

The biggest deterrent to successful arm timing in forward and reverse takeoffs is starting the arm swing too late in the drop from the top of the hurdle to the board. This point is key in making the press and takeoff work properly.

FULCRUM SETTING

When the diver is using the forward approach, you should set the fulcrum as far back as possible yet still allow the diver to land softly on the board after the hurdle. Correct timing means that as the feet make contact with the board, it is starting its downward motion.

Once a young or beginning diver learns the fundamental movements of the approach and can take off with good balance, move the fulcrum to the point just described. The earlier a diver is forced to use a slower board, the more easily he or she will achieve good diving rhythm.

You should periodically test all divers to find out if they can utilize the board effectively with the fulcrum set farther back. Divers can learn to adjust to progressively slower motion of the board, but if the diver is not challenged to do so, progress stops.

The backward press creates a different problem when you are determining where to set the fulcrum. Because the diver's feet do not leave the board during the springing motion, finding the point where the diver is not in rhythm with the board is more difficult than in the forward approach. However, the ideal fulcrum setting for the backward press is the setting at which the diver achieves the greatest height from the board. By moving the fulcrum to various settings and observing the diver performing a back jump, you can find this point.

As with the forward approach, test the diver periodically to see if he or she can effectively use the board with the fulcrum set back more than normally. Changes in the diver's size and strength may allow the use of a slower fulcrum setting, which will thus help the diver achieve more height on takeoff.

COMMON BACKWARD TAKEOFF MISTAKES AND CORRECTIONS

Mistake	Correction
The diver bends forward and shifts the balance forward.	Hold a stick or pole across the front of the diver, a few inches from the diver's chest during the press. As soon as the diver's arms swing down near the hips, remove the pole.
The diver circles the arms too far behind the body in the downswing.	Hold a stick or pole across the back of the diver at the appropriate distance to keep the arms from going too far back. Remove the pole when the arms pass below the level of the pole.
The diver circles the arms back and down too early, or excessively bends the arms.	Make the diver touch the sides of the knees with the fingertips at the bottom of the press.
The diver's arms are too late getting through the pressing motion.	Instruct the diver to start the arms down and back at the top of the press just before the legs begin bending. The diver should lift the arms to a lower position at the top of the press.

(Cont.)

COMMON BACKWARD TAKEOFF
MISTAKES AND CORRECTIONS (Continued)

Mistake	Correction
The diver's distance from the board is too great when the diver does any backward press.	See if the diver's heels drop below horizontal in the preliminary rocking motion or at the bottom of the press. Hold a pole across and in front of the board a foot farther away from the board than you want the diver to land. Have the diver do the press and whatever dive desired between the pole and the board. Obviously, you should move the pole if the diver is going to hit it, but don't tell the diver you intend to do that. Also, hold the pole across the diver's shoulders until his or her arms reach the top of the press, then remove the pole. This ensures that the diver does not lean away early or move the arms back too far in the upward movement. This also works great for keeping inward dives in good balance.

SUMMARY

Dry-land training on the movements of the forward approach and backward press must be practiced extensively. Using the training methods presented, the diver should be able to correctly perform the sequence of movements for both of these skills at normal execution speed. Only then should you have the diver perform the forward approach and backward press on the springboard in the pool.

3
CHAPTER

BASIC SKILLS AND DIVES

Once the diver learns the correct techniques of the forward approach and backward press, he or she needs to spend considerable time practicing forward and backward jumps and the four basic dives (forward, backward, reverse, and inward) in the tuck position before learning these dives in the pike position, and then in the straight position.

The training program for all levels of divers, not just for the beginner, should include work on these skills throughout the diver's career. These jumps and dives form the foundation for sound takeoffs and effective board use in all other dives. A diver who cannot perform an optional dive with the proper angle of takeoff, elevation in the air, and distance from the board most likely cannot execute a good jump or tuck dive in that direction of rotation.

FORWARD AND BACKWARD JUMPS

When performed in the straight position from the 1- and 3-meter springboards, these jumps provide excellent training in achieving full use of the board, good balance, and control of distance from the board.

The objective, after the diver completes the press and extension from the board, is to leave the board at a slightly forward angle of takeoff with the body in a straight line, with the arms straight and parallel overhead and in line with the body (see Figure 3.1, a and b). The balance and angle of takeoff should be such that the diver can hold this position without movement during the flight of the jump. For the forward jump, the diver should enter the water 3 to 4 feet from the board. For the backward jump, the entry should be at a distance, allowing the diver to reach out and touch the tip of the board. Poor boardwork will make it hard for the diver to perform these jumps well.

Figure 3.1 Straight-line takeoff in forward (a) and backward (b) directions.

ACTION–REACTION

Before beginning the discussion of takeoffs, we must understand the principle of action–reaction. Newton's third law of motion states that for every action there is an equal and opposite reaction. Applied to diving, this means if a diver pushes against the board in one direction with an amount of force, a resultant equal force from the board will occur in the opposite direction. If in midair the diver rotates the head in one direction, the feet and body will rotate in the opposite direction. Although explaining the physics of diving is not the purpose of this book, you need a general understanding of this concept for the next section, as well as in other areas of discussion.

TAKEOFFS

In springboard diving there are four basic takeoff directions: forward, backward, reverse, and inward. The coach and diver must understand how these are performed in order to obtain good balance and distance and to create adequate rotation to complete the dive.

In the previous chapter, the section on the basic takeoff position stated that all dives begin from the same body position prior to the recoil of the board, and what happens after that depends on the dive to be performed. One key point to keep in mind is that even though the basic takeoff position is the same for all dives with regard to the relationship of the legs, body, and arms, the point where the center of balance is maintained changes depending on the direction and amount of rotation involved.

Because this chapter deals only with the basic dives, the explanation of the takeoffs will relate to performance of those dives. Further discussion specific to optional dives is found in the somersault chapter (chapter 5).

Forward Dive Takeoffs

As the diver lands on the board from the hurdle, the body should be vertical, with the center of balance over the front of the feet. After the diver completes the press and the board begins its upward movement, the diver's body extends to a straight line, with the center of balance forward so the body leaves the board at an angle slightly forward of vertical. This position provides proper distance from the board (3 to 4 feet) and adequate rotation for the basic dives. Figure 3.2 illustrates how the upward thrust of the board (A) causes the diver to travel away from the board (B) and creates rotation in the forward direction (C).

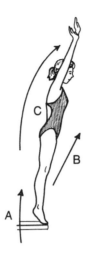

Figure 3.2 Forward straight-line takeoff.

When using the 1- and 3-meter boards, some divers who lack height in the air or who lack strength may need to create more rotation to complete the dive than occurs in the takeoff just described. A forward motion of the arms, head, and torso as one unit into a pike position prior to takeoff will create this rotation. As illustrated in Figure 3.3, the forward motion of the upper body (A) as the legs extend causes a forward push of the feet into the board (B); the board then pushes backward against the feet (C), creating a forward rotational movement (D). Because of the direction of the resultant force of the board against the feet, the diver's body will travel backward (E) as the body rotates forward. Therefore, the more forward rotation the diver creates, the more forward balance of the body is necessary to compensate for the increased backward travel, and to achieve good distance. This direction of body movement is minimal in the basic dives, because the rotational force needed is small. Thus, a diver need use only a slight forward lean in basic dives to compensate for the backward body movement and to assure good distance.

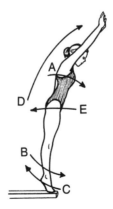

Figure 3.3 Forward pike action takeoff forces.

Inward Dive Takeoffs

The motions a diver needs in order to achieve good distance and rotation from an inward takeoff position are the same as those needed in the forward dives. Figure 3.4 shows that the piking movement of the body (A) occurs prior to takeoff, causing the feet to push forward against the board (B) and causing the board's force to be backward against the feet (C), creating rotation in the inward direction (D).

As explained for the forward takeoff, the direction of force from the board causes the diver to travel backward (E). With the inward takeoff, however, this means that the forces that create rotation also push the diver away from the board. For this reason the diver must maintain balance over the toes until these forces are applied, which occurs very late in the press—just before the diver leaves the board. Notice in Figure 3.4 how the upper body is still over the board as the feet are just about to lose contact with the board.

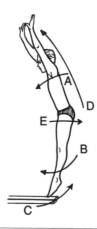

Figure 3.4   Inward takeoff forces.

If the diver loses balance in the backward direction before the rotational force and resulting movement away from the board occur, two things will happen.

1. Little rotation or elevation will result because the weight of the body will not be over the legs and in line with the force of the board at takeoff.
2. The diver will be too far away from the board due to the combination of backward lean and backward movement from the rotation actions.

If the diver maintains balance too far forward over the board, he or she can come too close to the board or strike the board. The diver will not achieve a safe distance from the board if his or her center of balance is located forward at a distance greater than the rotational force can move the diver backward when rotation is developed.

In order for the diver to achieve the proper takeoff, the center of balance should not move either forward or backward in the press. To further ensure good distance and rotation, the diver should think of keeping the upper body stationary while developing the piking motion prior to takeoff by driving the hips up and back with the legs, rather than keeping the hips stationary and driving the upper body forward and down. This is the major difference between the actions of the inward and forward takeoffs; the latter requires the diver to move the upper body forward when piking in order to develop more lean.

Backward Dive Takeoffs

To achieve good distance in the backward takeoff dives, the diver needs to move the center of balance backward in the press and extension prior to the takeoff. This leaning motion should not occur at the top of the press; if it does, the dive will be initiated with the whole body falling back, and the diver will lose control of balance. Instead, as the diver moves through the bottom of the press and begins to extend upward, he or she should shift the weight backward through the hips and legs while keeping the upper body over the tip of the board.

As the diver extends up to a straight body line for takeoff into the backward dive (see Figure 3.5), this shift of balance should account for an angle of takeoff sufficient for good distance and adequate rotation, the same as illustrated for the forward takeoff.

Figure 3.5 Backward straight-line takeoff.

If the diver needs added rotation to complete the back dive (especially in the straight position), he or she should arch the body prior to takeoff. As shown in Figure 3.6, the backward motion of the body (A) as the legs extend causes a backward push of the feet into the board (B); the board pushes forward against the feet (C), creating a backward rotational motion (D). This forward pushing force of the board also causes the body to travel toward the board (E). Because developing backward rotation causes the diver to move toward the board, the more rotation the diver creates, the more he or she needs a backward balance of the body to overcome this movement toward the board and to obtain proper distance.

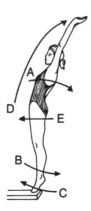

Figure 3.6 Backward arched takeoff forces.

Reverse Dive Takeoffs

The movements and direction of forces needed to create rotation in reverse dives are the same as for the backward dives. Figure 3.7 illustrates these forces. The arch of the body created as the diver pushes the hips up and forward (A) as the legs extend causes a backward push of the feet against the board (B) and an equal force from the board pushing forward against the feet (C). The force of the board creates reverse rotation (D), and the body travels forward in the direction of that force (E).

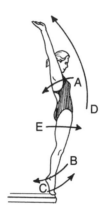

Figure 3.7 Reverse takeoff forces.

Because of this movement away from the board caused by the forces of reverse rotation, the diver can drop from the hurdle to the board with the balance slightly behind vertical, and safe distance will result. Emphasize that the diver should execute the arching movement by keeping the upper body still and driving the hips upward and forward. The opposite action—keeping the hips still and pulling the upper body backward and downward—will shift the center of balance back over the board, causing the diver to have insufficient distance.

As is the case with the inward takeoff, the balance should not move either forward or backward during the press but should remain steady until the force of the board moves the diver outward.

BASIC DIVES IN TUCK POSITION

The diving table used in competition assigns the forward, backward, reverse, and inward dives in tuck position lower degrees of difficulty than the same dives in pike or straight position. This would seem to indicate that tuck dives are easier to perform; however, these dives are really much more demanding. The tuck dives require more effective balance, body control, and use of the springboard than their counterparts.

To perform the tuck dives well, the diver must have complete body extension and arm reach, excellent body alignment, and near-perfect angle of takeoff. These dives are so delicate that the slightest out-of-control position or movement will result in poor execution.

Forward Dive

The diver performs the takeoff for this dive with the body straight; the arms are extended overhead, shoulder-width apart and in line with the body. The head should be level and the eyes should look straight ahead. The correct angle of takeoff will allow for good distance and proper rotation without any arm, head, or body motion in the forward direction during takeoff. The diver merely needs to stretch upward in a straight line and let the springboard do the rest.

After the feet leave the board, the diver gradually assumes the tuck position by bending at the waist and knees, drawing the thighs to the chest, bringing the heels to the buttocks, bending the elbows, and bringing the arms down to grasp the midpoint of the lower legs (shins). The chin should drop slightly, and the eyes should begin to focus on the entry point. The diver should achieve the completed tuck position just prior to the peak of the dive.

At the top of the dive the body begins its gradual opening. As the diver descends to the water, the body extends to a straight line, and the arms straighten and move laterally in line with the body to the overhead entry position (see Figure 3.8, a-f).

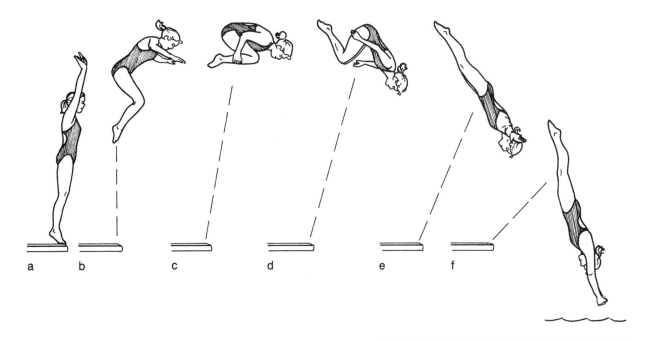

Figure 3.8   Forward dive tuck with lateral come-out.

Inward Dive

The actions of this dive in the air are the same as those for the forward dive tuck; however, because the inward dive tuck uses a different takeoff, the diver makes different motions while leaving the board to achieve proper distance and rotation.

As the arms complete their overhead reach and the body extends from the board, the diver first moves to a straight line of the body and arms. As the board recoils and propels the diver upward, the arms and torso hold their positions while the hips are driven backward and upward, causing a pike position just before takeoff. This motion moves the body away from the board and begins the inward rotation. The diver should keep the head level and still during the takeoff and should focus the eyes on the back end of the board or the wall behind the board (see Figure 3.9, a-f).

Unlike the forward dive tuck, in which the diver can keep the body and arms in a straight line and let the angle of the takeoff bring about good distance and rotation, the inward dive tuck requires the diver to change body shape to accomplish distance and rotation. Studying the explanation of inward takeoffs will help you understand these motions.

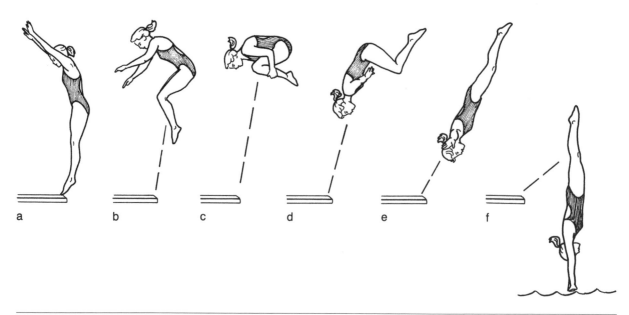

Figure 3.9   Inward dive tuck with lateral come-out.

Backward Dive

Most beginning diving students learn a basic backward dive first in the straight position. For ease of teaching, to reduce fear, and to eliminate the possibility of the diver's landing flat on the water, a coach will usually teach a diver initially to put the head back, look for the water with the eyes, and arch the back (see Figure 3.10, a and b). There is nothing wrong with this method; it does get the student to perform the dive more readily. However, as soon as the diver passes this initial learning stage you need to introduce a new technique of performing the backward entry, with the ultimate goal being to teach the diver a good backward dive tuck.

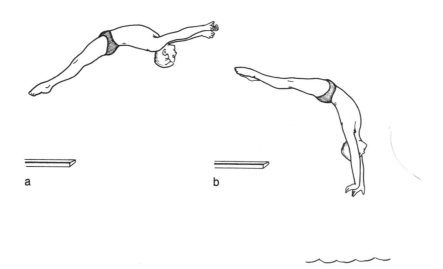

Figure 3.10   Arched backward dive.

Backward Slide-In (Straight)

To begin this process, you need a folding floor mat or exercise mat 5 or 6 feet in width. Fold this and place it lengthwise on the end of the 1-meter board; throw some water on the mat to make it slippery.

Instruct the diver to lie faceup on the mat with the head toward the pool and the arms extended overhead in line with the body, hands together. The diver should keep the head in a neutral position with the eyes looking toward the water. The diver lifts the heels slightly off the mat, keeping the legs straight, and you lift the foot end of the mat high enough (approximately 45 degrees) for the diver to slide into the water. The diver must hold the starting position throughout the dive, with no movement of the head backward or any arch in the body (see Figure 3.11, a-c). The diver will not be able to see the water at the point of entry but should see the water as close to the entry point as possible without tilting the head back. This is true of all the backward and reverse entries, from the basic through the optional dives.

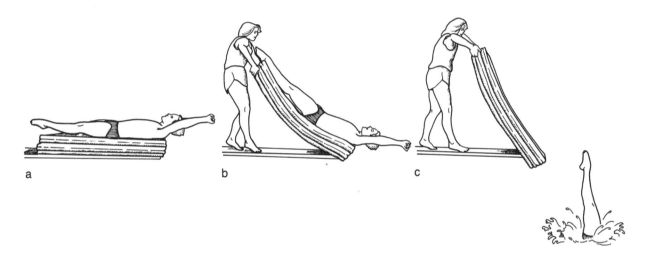

Figure 3.11 Backward slide-in.

Backward Slide-In (Lateral Arms)

When the diver can hold the body line straight throughout the dive, he or she should then try the slide-in with the arms straight and lateral at shoulder height in the starting position. The head tilts forward with the chin in, the upper body curls slightly, and the eyes look down the body to the elevated toes. The diver watches the toes as the slide begins. As the diver leaves the mat, he or she brings the arms laterally to the entry position, while the head moves to a neutral position and the eyes look back toward the water (see Figure 3.12, a-d).

The diver must repeat this drill frequently so that this body and head alignment becomes the ''natural'' way for the diver to enter the water backward. Even the highly skilled diver can benefit from periodic practice of this drill to maintain a good backward and reverse entry technique.

Performing this drill from the 3-meter board is an excellent way for more advanced divers to practice a straight line of entry for backward and reverse dives.

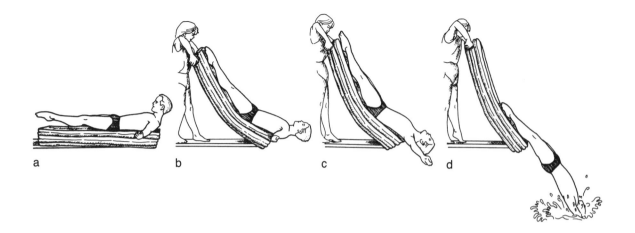

Figure 3.12 Backward slide-in with lateral arms.

It is impossible for the diver to enter the water vertically from this height if any arch in the body occurs or if the head is moved back to the neutral position prior to leaving the mat. Sliding in from this height also forces the diver to hold the correct position (slightly piked position at the hips, the upper body curled, with the head forward looking at the toes) for a longer time in the drop before preparing for the entry.

Backward Slide-In (Tuck)

Again using the 1-meter board, have the diver lie faceup on the mat, in a tuck position. When you lift the mat and the diver slides to the edge, he or she should open the body for the entry. The diver should stretch the body to the same line as practiced in the backward slide-in: straight, head held in a neutral position, and eyes looking back toward the water. As the diver opens from the tuck, the arms move from their position on the middle of the lower legs up the midline of the body; the elbows bend and the hands stay close together, and then the arms extend for the entry as they pass head level (see Figure 3.13, a-e).

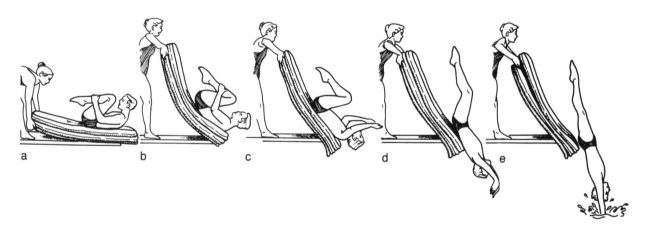

Figure 3.13 Backward slide-in in tuck position.

Backward Roll-Off (Tuck)

Position the mat so it overhangs the end of the 1-meter board a couple of inches, and have the diver sit in a tuck position, back facing the water, and hips at the edge of the mat. The diver rocks backward and opens for the entry just as he or she leaves the mat (see Figure 3.14, a-e). Caution the diver to kick the legs up toward a vertical line. The diver must also maintain the same entry position as in the previous drills and must stretch the arms the same way as for the slide-in in tuck position.

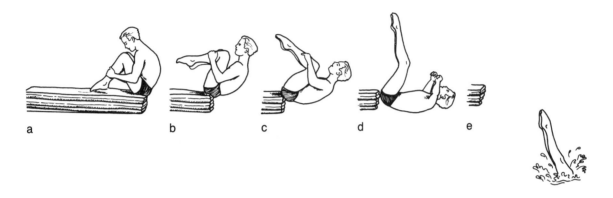

a   b   c   d   e

Figure 3.14 Backward roll-off in tuck position.

Once the diver can perform the backward roll-off in tuck position well and can do a backward press with a jump an arm's length from the board, it is time to perform the backward dive tuck. This is the most difficult of the tuck dives to master, because there is a strong tendency for divers to have too much angle of takeoff (backward lean) or too much arch in the body on takeoff. Both these situations cause excessive rotation, and a lack of control results.

As the diver leaves the board, the body should be in a straight line and the arms should be straight, parallel, and overhead in line with the body (see Figure 3.15). A slight angle of takeoff is needed to provide safe distance and proper rotation. In order to control the jump and counteract the tendency to rotate too fast, the diver should keep the head level but pushed forward of the body and arm line.

Figure 3.15 Takeoff position for backward dive tuck.

When the feet leave the board, the diver keeps the upper body and head still while the legs and arms bend and move to a tuck position during the ascent to the peak of the dive. Just before starting the drop to the water, the diver extends the legs and arms to a straight line for the entry. In this beginning stage the diver should bring the arms up the midline of the body with elbows bent and hands close together, then should straighten the arms as they pass the head (see Figure 3.16, a-f).

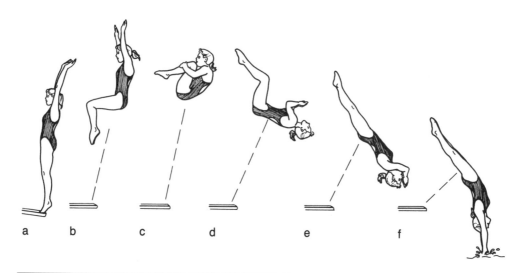

Figure 3.16   Backward dive tuck with straight-line come-out.

After the diver gains good control of the takeoff and dive rotation, he or she needs to learn another more advanced method of coming out of the tuck position. This method relates to the backward slide-in in straight position performed from the 3-meter board; that drill will help most in perfecting this backward dive tuck technique.

At the top of the backward dive tuck when the opening begins, the diver straightens the legs at the knee joint while the hips are not fully extended and the

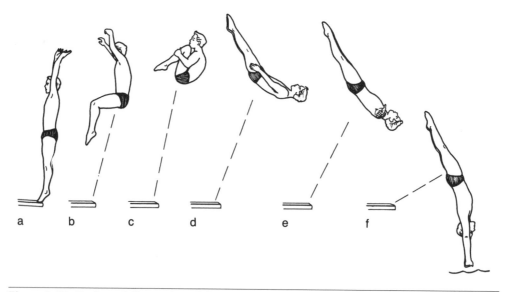

Figure 3.17   Backward dive tuck with lateral come-out.

body is in a pike position. The arms straighten simultaneously with the legs, and the diver moves the arms to a lateral placement at thigh level. The upper body remains curled just as it was in the tuck position, and the head stays forward with the chin in, eyes looking at the toes (as with the backward slide-in from a 3-meter board). When the diver establishes this position, the body extends at the hips to a straight line, and the arms begin to move laterally to the overhead entry position, while the head tilts back to a neutral position and the eyes look back toward the water (see Figure 3.17, a-f).

Reverse Dive

The mechanics of execution for this dive are exactly the same as for the backward dive tuck; once the diver can perform the backward dive tuck well, the reverse dive tuck should be no problem. In fact, with the exception of the takeoff, the reverse dive tuck is much easier to control.

The diver gains proper distance from the board during the backward dive tuck by having a slight backward angle from the board. For the reverse dive tuck, the diver moves out to a good distance of 3 to 4 feet from the board by pushing the hips forward and upward, causing a body arch as the diver extends and reaches up with the arms after the press. This hip motion moves the center of gravity forward, and therefore the body moves away from the board. The body arch that occurs while the diver is still in contact with the board also helps him or her gain rotation for the dive (see Figure 3.18, a-g). Obviously, too much hip and body motion will cause the diver to move too far out and rotate too fast. Consult the section on reverse dive takeoffs for a more extensive explanation of this technique.

Unfortunately, other than practicing on a trampoline or dry-land board, with an overhead spotting apparatus, the diver has no feasible drills with which to practice this dive. Learning a good backward dive tuck and good forward approach with front jump and combining the two are the best methods of learning this dive.

When the diver can execute tuck dives with balance and control, he or she is ready to learn the remaining basic dives. It is best for the diver to progress from tuck to pike and, when the pike dives are done well, then to straight position. Attempting the straight dives too soon can cause the diver to lose good takeoff and body line techniques. For this reason, the pike dives are presented next.

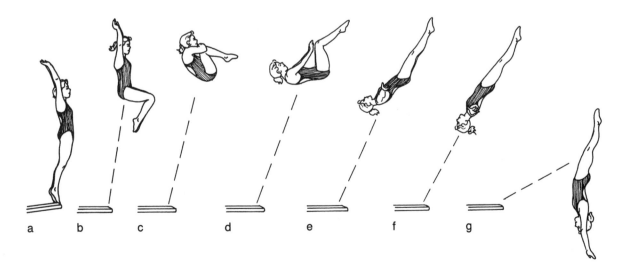

Figure 3.18 Reverse dive tuck with lateral come-out.

BASIC DIVES IN PIKE POSITION

The technique of takeoff and initiating rotation are the same for the tuck and pike dives. Because the diver rotates slower in the pike position, more rotational force will be needed to complete these dives.

Forward Dive

The takeoff position for this dive is the same as for the forward dive tuck. As the diver leaves the board the eyes focus on a point at the far end of the pool. Just after the takeoff, keeping the legs straight, the diver begins moving the arms down the front of the body, and the body bends at the waist so that at the peak of the dive, the hands touch the feet in a pike position. As the diver performs the pike, the eyes change focus from the far end of the pool to the entry point. Just as the diver begins descending, he or she opens up the body in preparation for the entry by extending at the hips, bringing the body to a straight alignment, and moving the arms laterally to the entry position (see Figure 3.19, a-e).

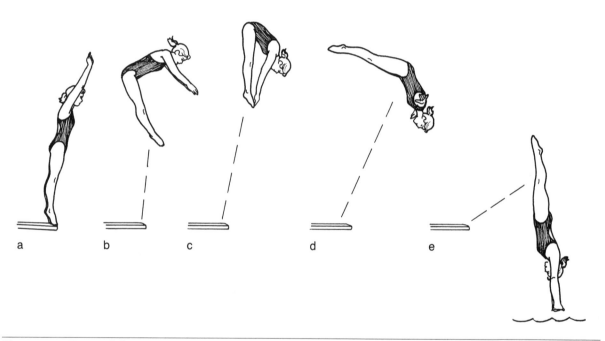

a   b   c   d   e

Figure 3.19 Forward dive pike.

Inward Dive

The movements of this dive in the air are the same as for the forward dive pike. As we noted for the inward dive tuck, just before the diver leaves the board, the legs push the hips upward and back, causing the body to pike; this moves the body away from the board to a safe distance and creates rotation for the dive (see Figure 3.20, a-e).

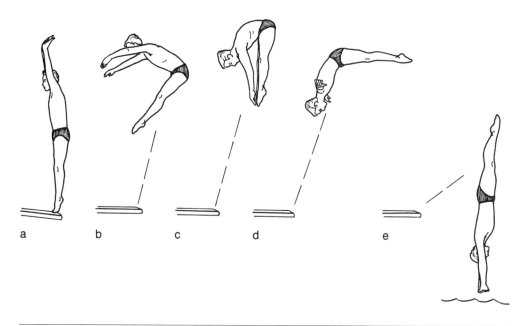

Figure 3.20 Inward dive pike.

Backward Dive

At the takeoff point, the diver extends the body to a straight line at an angle slightly backward of vertical. The arms are straight, parallel, and stretched at the shoulder joint so they reach overhead in line with the body. The head is level but pressed forward, as described for the backward dive tuck, for balance and control. The eyes look straight ahead, waiting for the legs to come into view as the diver lifts the legs into the pike.

Immediately after the diver leaves the board, the legs begin to lift into a pike position as the arms move forward in front of the body to touch the feet at an angle short of vertical. The angle of touch varies, depending on the amount of rotation, the height from the board, and whether the diver is using the 1- or 3-meter board. As the arms and legs come together, the eyes follow the feet to the touch position and the diver positions the head between the arms so the top of the shoulders are pressed against the ears.

Following the touch, the diver moves the arms laterally (palms facing the feet) in line with the body, as the body begins to open from the pike at the hip joint. The upper body remains in a concave, curled position with the eyes focused on the feet. This is the same opening position described for the backward dive tuck. As the body reaches full extension of the hip joint, the diver straightens the back and tilts the head back to a neutral position so the body is in a straight line. The diver times the lateral movement of the arms so they are at shoulder level when this occurs. This point in the drop to the water is seen as a T body position.

As the diver continues to descend, he or she closes the arms laterally overhead for the entry while maintaining the body's straight line (see Figure 3.21, a-f).

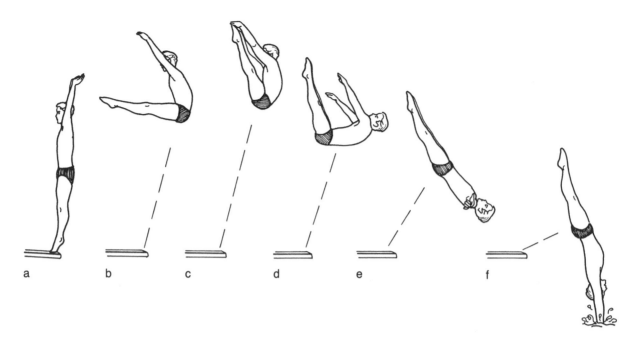

Figure 3.21 Backward dive pike.

Reverse Dive

The reverse dive pike is executed much like the backward dive pike. The difference occurs during the reverse dive pike takeoff, when a forward and upward motion of the hips causes a slight body arch at the point of takeoff; this arch enables the diver to move to the correct distance and develop the rotation needed to complete the dive (see Figure 3.22, a-f).

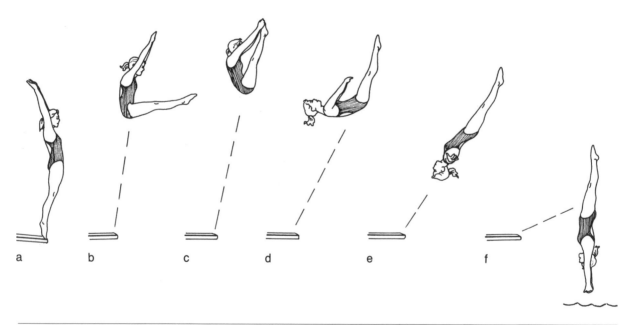

Figure 3.22 Reverse dive pike.

BASIC DIVES IN STRAIGHT POSITION

After the diver can execute the tuck and pike dives well, he or she should be able to learn the straight dives easily and correctly, with good balance, control, and most importantly a straight body line throughout the dive.

Forward Dive

The takeoff position for this dive is the same as for the forward dives tuck and pike, except that the body is angled slightly more forward from the board, to create the added rotation needed to complete the dive. A diver using the 1-meter board, and especially a smaller, young diver who doesn't go as high in the air, may need to develop more rotation than is obtained with the body straight. If just prior to leaving the board the diver presses the arms and upper body slightly forward, causing a pike at the hips, added rotation will result. As soon as the diver leaves the board, he or she should straighten the body. In order to keep the head level, the diver should focus the eyes on the far side of the pool as the diver rises to the top of the dive. The common tendency is for the diver to look at the entry point during this phase of the dive, which causes the head to drop. This head position doesn't look good and, it may create a pike in the body.

As soon as the feet leave the board, the arms move laterally in line with the body, down to shoulder level. The diver should reach this position as soon as possible, but not in a rushed or jerky movement. Certainly the diver should establish this T alignment before reaching the top of the elevation.

From the time just before the diver reaches the top of the dive until the descent to the water begins, there should be no movement of the body parts, only rotation of the body forward as a single unit. At the peak of the dive, the diver's eyes move from their focus on the far side of the pool to the entry point on the water, obviously with no head motion. As the diver drops to the water, the arms move laterally to the overhead entry position (see Figure 3.23, a-e).

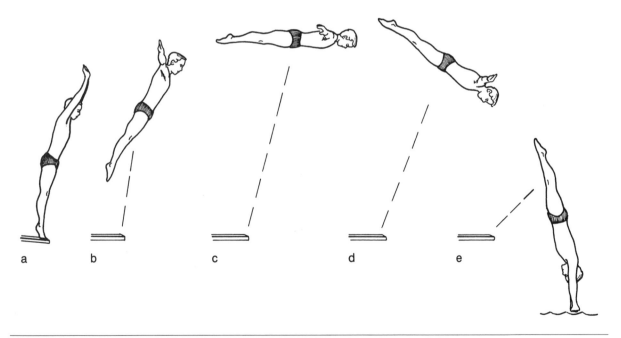

a   b   c   d   e

Figure 3.23 Forward dive straight.

Inward Dive

This dive is best learned from the 3-meter board first. The added height makes it easier for the diver to complete the dive using good technique. Once the diver establishes the correct execution pattern, the dive can be transferred to the 1-meter board.

The basic movements of this dive in the air are the same as for the forward dive straight. In order for the diver to move the dive to safe distance and develop the necessary rotation, as in the inward dive tuck and pike, the legs must push the hips up and back causing a piked body position prior to takeoff. As soon as the feet leave the board, the diver extends the body to a straight position as the arms begin their lateral motion (see Figure 3.24, a-e).

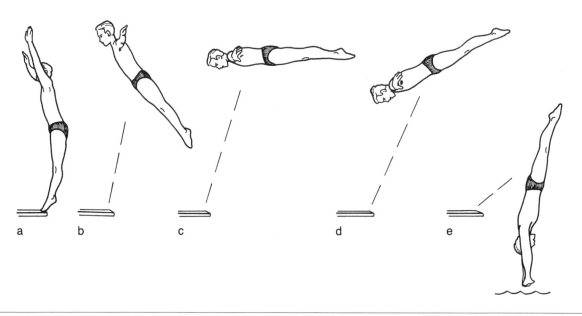

a   b   c   d   e

Figure 3.24   Inward dive straight.

Divers who are very young, do not possess good strength, or cannot maintain proper balance during the takeoff, develop a pronounced pike for a considerable time period after leaving the board. These divers also tend to drop their heads very low throughout the flight of the dive. The overall result is a poor dive. A diver who has such a problem should not perform this dive until the factor causing the problem is corrected. For the balance problem, more work on backward jumps and inward dive tuck is indicated. In the other cases, maturation, an exercise program, or both are needed.

Backward Dive

The takeoff position for this dive is a straight line through the body with the head level, eyes looking up, and the arms straight and shoulder-width apart in an overhead position in line with the body. Some divers may find a slight arch necessary in order to complete the rotation easily. The angle of the body during takeoff should be slightly more than for the backward dive pike. When the feet leave the board, the arms move laterally down to shoulder level before the diver reaches the top of the dive.

The head and body remain still during the whole dive. The diver should maintain a motionless T position through the middle third of the dive, that is, from before until after the peak of the dive. During the drop to the water, the arms close laterally to the overhead entry position. Throughout the flight of the dive, the eyes should not focus on any one point, because this will cause a head movement. Instead, the eyes should look up until the diver can see the water as the dive approaches the entry (see Figure 3.25, a-e). As noted before, the diver should sight the water as close to the entry point as possible without tilting the head back.

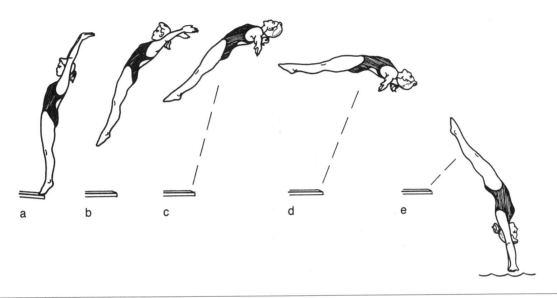

Figure 3.25 Backward dive straight.

Reverse Dive

As with the reverse dives tuck and pike, this dive is performed much like the backward dive; the difference is that during the reverse dive straight, the hips push forward and upward, creating a slightly arched body position on takeoff for distance and rotation purposes (see Figure 3.26, a-f).

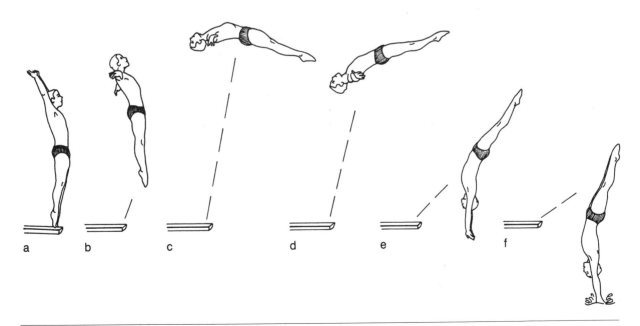

Figure 3.26 Reverse dive straight.

Forward Dive With 1/2 Twist

Even though this dive is not a basic dive requirement in most levels of diving, there are some instances in which a diver may need to perform this dive because of a lack of other twisting dive choices.

Just before the feet leave the board, as the diver holds the body straight and the arms reach overhead, the shoulders begin a gradual turn in the desired direction of twist. Let's assume that the diver is twisting left, which means the right shoulder moves forward and the left one backward. This movement initiates the twist from the board. As the feet leave the board, the diver moves the arms laterally down to shoulder level and focuses the eyes on the far side of the pool, just as in the forward dive straight. The diver should achieve the arm position prior to the peak of the dive; the speed of twist should be such that at the top of the dive, the leading arm (right arm in this case) points at the entry spot, the other arm points at the ceiling directly above the entry spot, and the diver is in a 1/4-twist position. When the diver achieves this position, he or she brings the chin down and in line with the right shoulder, with the eyes sighting down the arm and hand to the entry point.

As the legs rotate upward and the body continues to twist during the descent, the right arm continues to point at the entry and the eyes sight down the arm to that point, while the left arm remains still. In holding this position, the diver will automatically complete the 1/2 twist and the right arm will close overhead while the head rotates back to a neutral position. Prior to closing for the entry, the diver stretches the right arm overhead and holds the left arm lateral at shoulder level. At this point the diver brings the left arm laterally overhead to join the right arm for the entry. Essentially, this means the diver prepares for the entry one arm at a time; first the right arm closes overhead, then the left arm. When the left arm begins its closing motion, the head should gradually move from its slightly backward position into alignment with the body.

It is extremely important that during the drop from the peak of the dive, the right arm points at the entry spot and the eyes do not lose sight of the arm on the entry point (see Figure 3.27, a-e).

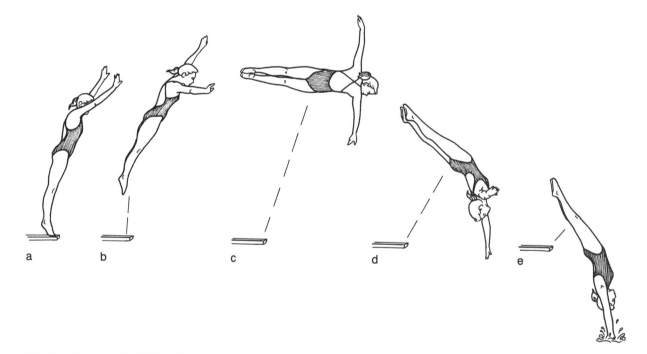

Figure 3.27 Forward dive with 1/2 twist straight.

SUMMARY

Practice on the basic dives in the tuck, pike, and straight positions should take place at the same time as training on the skills presented in the next chapter. Entry, lineup, and come-out techniques complement the basic dives well, by teaching the diver how to complete dives accurately.

4
CHAPTER

HEADFIRST ENTRIES, LINEUPS, AND COME-OUTS

Why discuss entry before considering any of the optional dives? The reason is that divers should learn the correct headfirst entry technique and methods of practice as soon as possible after learning the basic dives. Diligent, long-term training for good entries brings about better body alignment in all phases of diving, a keen sense of vertical completion of dives, and an opportunity to practice the various methods of coming out of basic and somersaulting dives.

Divers seem to enjoy practicing entries because they require less energy than the dives themselves, entries focus on one particular skill, and improvement can be rapid. It is important to devote some portion of daily practice to entry work, and on some days it is worthwhile to devote the whole practice to this skill training.

COMMON ELEMENTS

There are two types of headfirst entry: forward and backward. The forward entry is used for all forward, inward, and multiple-twisting dives, whereas the backward entry is employed in all backward and reverse dives. No matter in which direction or with which dive an entry is performed, there are certain fundamentals common to all entries.

Body Alignment

The same basic hip, torso, and head positions discussed in chapter 1 form the foundation of a good forward or backward entry. This alignment provides stability through the body when the force of entry impact occurs. Without good alignment, movement in these body areas takes place in the first 3 to 4 feet of entry, which results in a whiplash series of movements. Figure 4.1, a and b, shows the correct basic dive entry position; note the arm alignment in the entry position.

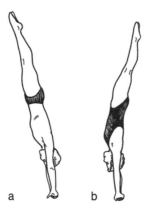

Figure 4.1 Correct basic dive entry position: (a) shows the forward inward stretch, and (b) shows the backward reverse stretch.

Hand Position

There is one element of hand position all experts will agree upon: The palm of the hand should make contact with the water first to initiate a good entry. Although there are variations, the most common and successful way for the diver to achieve this is to grab the back of one hand in the palm of the other with the thumbs interlocked and flexed so they are not sticking out for the water to pull on them. The lead hand (the one entering the water first) is open, with fingers extended and together and the palm area flat. The fingers of the grabbing hand should be together and securely wrapped around the back of the lead hand (see Figure 4.2).

Figure 4.2 Entry hand position.

Stretch Position

The lead hand should be positioned so that the palm is horizontal and the fingers point in a line parallel with the line of the shoulders. The diver should feel impact with the water "dead center" on the palm of the lead hand. The diver must elevate the shoulders and hold them tightly against the ears while locking the elbows. No movement in either the shoulder or elbow joints should occur during impact. A diver with hyperextended elbows can hold his or her position much more easily than can a diver with a straight elbow joint, or worse, an elbow joint that does not straighten completely.

When doing dives with a lateral line of closure for the entry, the diver should pronate the palms (so they face the feet) during this movement; this eliminates the need to rotate the palms in preparation for the correct hand position. Figure 4.3, a-c, illustrates this closing method and the correct stretch position.

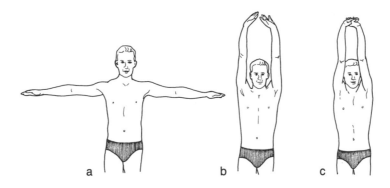

Figure 4.3 Entry stretch position.

Head Position and Vision

The diver should hold the head in a level position for all entries, which eliminates the possibility of looking directly at the entry point. *There should be no head movement during the entry.*

In forward and inward rotating dives and twisting dives, the diver can see the entry point at the beginning of the stretch because this point is located in front of the line of sight. However, after the diver sights this point and drops to the water, he or she should keep the head in the level position; the diver should look through the eyebrows to see as close to the entry point as possible without lifting the head.

In the backward and reverse entry, the diver cannot see the entry point because it is behind the line of sight. Again, the diver should keep the head level, looking as close to the actual entry point as possible without tilting the head backward.

Body Shape and Angle of Entry

Because the direction of rotation and the direction of stretching for the water are opposite for the forward and backward entries, the body shape and the way the arms stretch must change to account for the differences.

''Go with the flow of the dive'' best describes the most effective way to enter the water from any entry direction. This means the diver must utilize the arms, the body shape, and the direction of stretch through the shoulder joint to keep the body rotating through the water in the same direction as the dive rotation.

THE FORWARD ENTRY

Due to the direction of rotation of forward entries (i.e., forward, inward, and multiple-twisting dives), a pressure is created as the hands contact the water. This pressure tends to push the arms back overhead to a position behind the ears, which pulls the torso out of its body alignment to a position with the rib cage protruding forward; this causes an arch in the back and hyperextension across the hip joint. To compensate, the diver must first stretch the shoulder joint upward and with a forward pressure. Second, depending on the speed of rotation of the dive and the angle of entry, the diver may need to assume a ''hollow'' body configuration. This hollow position means that a line drawn from the hands through the body to the feet will be curved, because the body is in a concave alignment (see Figure 4.4).

In the basic forward and inward dives, the amount of rotation at entry is very small, and thus the angle of entry is close to vertical at impact. This means that

Figure 4.4   Forward dive with hollow stretch.

the diver needs a small amount of forward stretch pressure through the shoulder joint and a minimal or even an imperceptible degree of hollow body position in order to "go with the flow."

Figure 4.5   Forward 2-1/2 somersault with hollow stretch.

The optional dives, however, have far greater rotational force present at entry, and the angle of initial entry can be far short of vertical at times. These conditions dictate not only a strong forward direction of stretch at the shoulder joint, but a downward position of the head with the arms stretching in front of the body line. Also, the amount of hollow body configuration is significant (see Figure 4.5).

THE BACKWARD ENTRY

The backward and reverse rotating entries present the same set of circumstances as the forward entry, but forces occur in the opposite direction. As the diver enters, the water pressure pushes the arms forward; this can move the arms out of line in front of the face and throw the body into a pike action. To counteract this, the diver should stretch the arms backward at the shoulder joint and use a curvature of the body line or arched position on the back side of the body. It is important that the diver achieve the arched position through a stretching action across the hip joint while maintaining good body alignment in the upper body.

Arching the body backward by moving the rib cage off alignment causes the body to lose its rigidity on impact, resulting in a series of uncontrolled movements. This means that in addition to keeping the body arched, the diver must be sure that the muscles that maintain body alignment remain contracted.

As with the forward entry, the basic backward and reverse dives create a small amount of rotational force, and the angle of entry to the water is almost vertical. Therefore, the amount of backward stretch at the shoulder joint and the degree of body arch are minimal (see Figure 4.6).

Figure 4.6   Backward entry for basic dives.

The optional dives, due to their greater amount of rotational speed and resultant greater initial angle of entry short of vertical at impact, require a stronger backward stretch of the arms and more body arch. It is important that the amount of body arch does not become excessive, because when this occurs the appearance of the entry is poor and the diver loses control of the body during entry (see Figure 4.7).

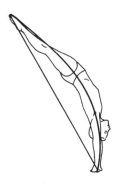

Figure 4.7   Backward entry for optional dives.

FORWARD VERSUS INWARD ENTRIES

The stretch and body alignment for these two entries are the same; however, the directions in which the dives move in relation to the water are opposite, causing different actions on the body.

In the forward dives, including forward and backward twisting dives, the body travels across the surface of the water in the same direction as the rotation of each dive (see Figure 4.8). This means that as the body contacts the water, the body's forward travel slows, causing a transfer of momentum through the upper body and to the legs. The result is a movement of the body toward overrotation.

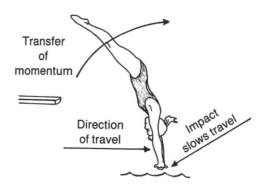

Figure 4.8 Forward entry rotational force.

In the inward dives, including reverse twisting dives, the body travels across the water in the opposite direction of the dive's rotation. Thus, when the body enters the water, the transfer of momentum through the body causes a movement toward underrotation (see Figure 4.9).

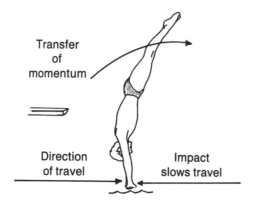

Figure 4.9 Inward entry rotational force.

This difference tells us that in general, in order to achieve a vertical finish of the dive, the diver must line up inward dives and reverse twisting dives closer to vertical than necessary for the forward dives and forward twisting and backward twisting dives.

BACKWARD VERSUS REVERSE ENTRIES

In the backward entry dives, the body travels across the water surface in the same direction in which the dive rotates; therefore, as in the forward rotating dives, the water pressure on the body causes a transfer of momentum through the torso and legs, which results in a movement toward overrotation (see Figure 4.10).

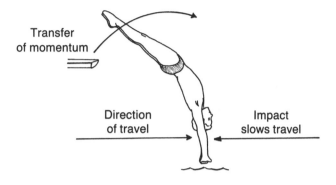

Figure 4.10 Backward entry rotational force.

The reverse dives are similar to the inward dives in that the diver travels in a direction opposite the rotation of the dive, thus causing a force on impact that moves the diver toward underrotation (see Figure 4.11). The reverse dive entries, therefore, must be lined up closer to vertical than the backward entry dives in order for the diver to achieve a vertical finish of the dive.

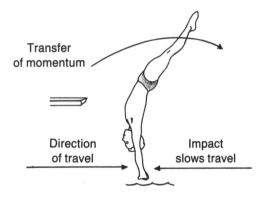

Figure 4.11 Reverse entry rotational force.

UNDERWATER TECHNIQUES

The beginning- and intermediate-level diver should practice the basic stretch position, holding it throughout the entry period and going to the bottom of the pool without any other movements. Before moving to the more advanced entry techniques presented here, the diver should demonstrate a good angle of entry in all directions along with a correct body line while doing the basic dives and lineup drills.

With a good body line and control of entry angle as the basic foundation, the diver can begin to change body shape and maneuver underwater to achieve a more consistent entry with less splash and to produce an accompanying unique sound. This type of entry is called a *rip,* because the sound is similar to that of ripping a piece of fabric. Even though some divers can rip an entry using only the fundamental stretch described previously and the flat palm position, most divers are more successful at mastering this skill with the following methods.

FORWARD SWIM AND SAVE

During the 1st foot of penetration into the water, the diver releases the grasp of the hands and starts a breaststroke-like swimming action in a direction 45 degrees in front of the body line. During this motion the arms must remain straight. If the diver performs this "swim" motion at the correct time and speed during the entry, the hands will stay very near the surface of the water as the body passes through. This will create a distinctive area of air and bubbles on each side of the entry.

As the hips pass through the surface, the head moves down and a pike occurs at the hips, causing the diver to roll over with the back to the bottom of the pool. This movement, called the forward somersault save, helps the legs enter the water on a vertical line. As the diver performs the pike, he or she must draw the legs toward the torso to prevent overrotation. The speed and force of the pike action depend on the angle of entry and the amount of rotation of the dive. Only through practice and experience can the diver learn to match the amount of "save" with the various dives and entry situations.

BACKWARD SWIM AND SAVE

As soon as the entry impact occurs, the diver releases the grasp of the hands and begins the swimming action of the arms during the 1st foot of entry. The diver swims with the arms straight and moving in a forward direction at a 45-degree angle to the body. When this is timed correctly the hands will stay very near the surface of the water for the first part of the entry.

As the hips pass through the water, the backward knee save starts as the head tilts backward and the body arches. When the knees pass through the water they are bent and the heels are pressed toward the hips while the body increases its arch and the head lifts toward the surface. The speed and force of the knee save depend on the angle of entry and amount of rotation of the dive. Experimentation with the different dives and the experience gained over a period of time will allow the diver to become very adept at keeping the angle of the legs and feet vertical at the finish of the entry.

TRAINING METHODS FOR ENTRIES

1. ***Hand position.*** Dry-land training drills can improve the diver's consistency in obtaining the correct hand position for entry. First, instruct the diver to perform the grabbing motion at a slow speed by holding the arms laterally at shoulder height with the palms facing backward. Keeping the arms straight, the diver should bring the hands together at shoulder height in front of the body. When the diver practices this way first, you and the diver can both visually check to see that the position is correct. As skill and familiarity with the correct grab increase, the diver can increase the speed of the closing movement. Next, the diver should practice the same drill to the overhead stretching position, maintaining good body alignment, keeping the head level, and looking toward the hands.

   When the diver attains proficiency with this drill, he or she can practice dives from the pool deck with the hands initially placed in the flat-palm stretching position, which aids in giving the feeling of the flat-hand entry. In the initial stages, the force on the hand created because of the larger landing surface may feel strange, and unstable movements of the body may occur, but both will pass in a short time. When accustomed to the feel of this entry, the diver can start the dive with the arms lateral at shoulder level and the palms down, and can close for the entry in midair. After several repetitions, the diver can try some dives from the 1-meter board.

Using the hand-grab dry-land drills in a daily warm-up routine will help the diver effectively and consistently achieve the correct hand position, which will be reflected in better entries.

2. **Swimming.** The diver stands in the entry stretch position, with a partner standing behind. The partner reaches up and taps the flat palm of the diver's leading hand in the same spot where the diver should feel the water contact the hand (center of palm). As quickly as possible the diver performs the swimming motion described previously. The participants repeat the drill several times, with the partner varying the time interval between taps, so the diver cannot anticipate when to swim but must rely on feeling the contact on the palm before reacting.

3. **Stability.** The participants start in the same position as the previous drill, except the partner stands on an elevated area (e.g., bench). The partner places both hands, one on top of the other, on the palm of the diver, then pushes down quickly and forcefully to simulate entry impact. The diver's goal is to hold the shoulders up tight against the ears and maintain alignment so that the impact force does not cause any movement in the back, hips, or knees. If such movement does occur, the body line is not straight and needs to be adjusted.

PRACTICING ENTRIES (LINEUPS)

Lineups are drills a diver can use for practicing the entry techniques just described without having to deal with the additional distracting influences of takeoffs and somersaulting momentum. Lineups allow the diver to focus solely on achieving correct angle of entry, correct body line, and control of the entry path while performing a variety of movements that directly relate to those needed in the basic and optional dives.

There are three types of lineup drills.

1. Entry (forward, backward)
2. Basic dive (forward, inward, backward, reverse)
3. Somersault come-outs (forward, inward, backward, reverse)

The diver should become proficient at each one, in the order presented here, before progressing to the next. Until the diver reaches an advanced level of entry skill, he or she should practice all three types of lineup regularly. The advanced diver can be more specific by practicing the lineups that relate to the dives being done in competition.

Entry Lineups

The purpose of these lineups is to isolate the forward and backward entry skills by making the movements involved as elementary as possible. The diver should practice these entries from the 3-meter springboard or platform. However, if neither is available the diver can use a 1-meter springboard and can generate a small spring with the legs only, which should provide the diver enough time and rotation to enter the water vertically. After the diver gains experience at the 3-meter height, he or she can practice these drills at the 5-meter level.

The forward entry technique is best practiced with a lineup named the forward hollow fall (see Figure 4.12, a-c). The diver stands on the end of the 3-meter board, maintaining a straight line at the hips with the upper body curled into the hollow position. The diver places the arms in the entry stretch overhead with the hands in the entry grab position and holds the head level with the chin down and in. The diver then stands up high on the toes and falls forward into the water, with no spring or body movements. As the diver enters the water, he or she holds the hollow position and maintains a forward direction of stretch through the shoulder joint. This drill is designed to teach the diver how to enter vertically while moving through the water smoothly in the direction of rotation (i.e., going with the flow).

Figure 4.12 Forward hollow fall from 3-meter height.

The diver practices the backward entry from the 3-meter board while performing a backward fall. The diver stands backward on the end of the board, with the arms overhead and the hands clasped in the entry position. The diver keeps the chin level with the eyes looking up. The body should have a slight arch at the hip joint, with the upper body kept in alignment. The diver then falls into a backward dive while holding the initial alignment (see Figure 4.13, a-d).

Figure 4.13 Backward fall with arms overhead from 3-meter height.

At first, this lineup may cause the diver to enter the water short of vertical, but with practice at how fast to initiate the falling speed from the board, the diver can accomplish a vertical finish. This drill allows the diver to learn the proper arm, head, upper body, and body arch position without any movement except the fall. It also teaches the diver to enter backward without tilting the head back and without looking directly at the entry point.

Basic Dive Lineups

When the diver learns the forward and backward entry techniques so he or she is consistent at lining up vertically, can control the body throughout the entry, and does not make an excessive amount of splash, the next level of practice can be started.

The basic dives (forward, backward, reverse, and inward) done in any of the positions are all completed with a lateral close of the arms to the overhead stretch for the entry. The diver needs to know how to line up correctly when rotating in the different directions and moving from the various body positions to the entry. These lineups are presented in the order in which they should be learned and practiced.

Forward Lineup

The best way for the diver to begin to learn a basic forward dive lineup is to practice the forward hollow fall in the straight position from the 3-meter board, with the arms held lateral during the fall and closed laterally for the entry during the drop to the water. When this is done effectively, the diver can start practice for the pike and tuck dives. The diver should learn the pike lineup first, because it involves fewer movements and is therefore easier.

The diver should initially practice the pike lineup from the 1-meter board by standing on the end, bent over into an open pike position. The diver stands up on the toes, falls forward, and opens to the straight position while closing the arms laterally to the entry stretch position (see Figure 4.14, a-d). Next, the diver can practice the same drill from the 3-meter board. When the diver can do this effectively, he or she should perform the same dive standing with a spring, from the 1-meter and then the 3-meter board.

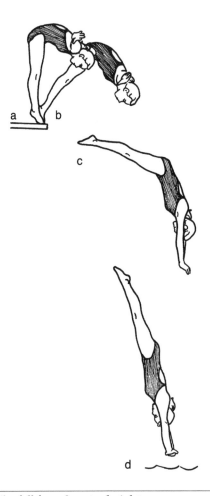

Figure 4.14 Forward open-pike fall from 3-meter height.

Forward tuck lineups are done standing and are performed with a spring. Using the 1-meter board, the diver performs a forward dive tuck with a lateral arm path while stretching for the entry. The diver can also perform a tuck lineup from the 3-meter board. The diver sits forward in a tuck position on the end of the board (see Figure 4.15, a-e). Staying in the tuck position, the diver rocks forward and begins rotating to the front dive position. Just as the hips leave the board, the

Figure 4.15 Forward tuck roll-off with lateral come-out from 3-meter height.

diver kicks out and lines up laterally with the arms, just as described in chapter 3 for the forward dive tuck.

The diver can best practice lining up from the straight position by using the 3-meter board. The diver stands forward at the end of the board with the arms held lateral at shoulder height; this is similar to the hollow fall dive described earlier, only the diver now holds the body in a straight alignment as done for a forward dive straight. The diver stands up on the toes and falls to a forward dive entry.

Inward Lineup

Because of the need to create rotation and move a safe distance from the board, the diver must practice these lineups with a backward press and spring. In addition, all should be done with a lateral stretching path for the entry. The sequence of drills to be practiced is this: the inward dive in the open pike position from the 1-meter board, the inward dive tuck from the 1-meter board, and then both dives from the 3-meter board.

Backward Lineup

The easiest method for the diver to practice the backward lineup is to perform a standing backward fall from the 3-meter board with arms held laterally at shoulder height. No spring is used. As the diver falls from the board, he or she closes the arms laterally overhead for the entry and moves the head to level as the eyes look back for the water. The body should have a slightly arched shape, with the arch coming from the hip area and not from the upper body. This curved position allows the diver to slide into the water smoothly (see Figure 4.16, a-d).

Figure 4.16   Backward fall, with arms lateral, from 3-meter height.

The diver can practice the same drill from the 1-meter board by taking a small spring with the legs into the takeoff; this allows the diver to complete the necessary rotation (see Figure 4.17, a-f). The 3-meter drill is preferred, especially for the less advanced diver, because less movement and rotation are involved, making concentration on body position and accuracy of entry easier.

When the diver can perform the back fall well, he or she can try the sitting tuck and pike roll-off from the 3-meter board next. The tuck position should be learned first.

The diver sits in a tuck position backward on the end of the board with the hips 2 to 3 inches from the tip (see Figure 4.18, a-e). Sitting this distance from the tip of the board aids in the rotation of the dive, because the board holds the hips up as the diver rotates backward. The diver rocks backward, staying in the tuck position until the hips leave the board. At this point the diver kicks the legs and performs a backward dive tuck come-out action as described in chapter 3. The diver can try this same drill in the open pike position, although balancing and holding the legs up in position require more skill and strength than needed for the tuck roll-off.

Figure 4.17   Backward lineup with arms lateral and with spring, from 1-meter height.

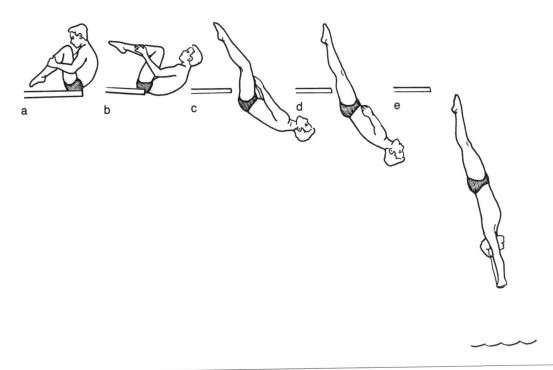

Figure 4.18   Backward tuck roll-off with lateral come-out, from 3-meter height.

If no 3-meter board is available, the diver can practice the backward lineup from the 1-meter board by doing a backward dive tuck as described earlier, or a backward dive open-pike as shown in Figure 4.19, a-e.

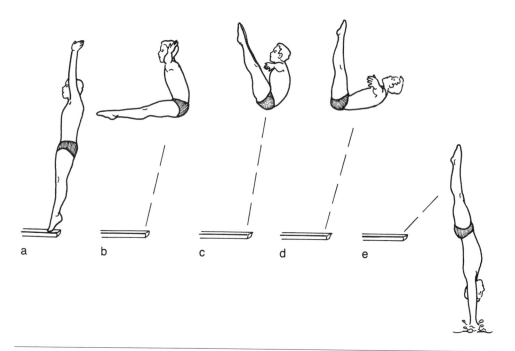

Figure 4.19   Backward dive open pike.

Reverse Lineup

Unfortunately, as with the inward lineup, these entries must be practiced with a spring. However, if the diver first masters a good backward lineup in the various drills presented, these entries will be relatively easy.

From the 1-meter board, the diver can first practice a standing reverse dive tuck and reverse dive open-pike with a spring, and then with a full forward approach. The same can be done from the 3-meter board.

Somersault Come-Out Lineups

The diver performs these lineups to simulate methods of coming out of somersault spins for a headfirst entry, while also learning to do a good entry with these movements.

For forward and inward somersault optionals in tuck or pike position, two come-out techniques are used.

Method	Description
1. Straight line.	The diver extends the legs and arms simultaneously to a straight line. The diver brings the arms from their position in the spin to the overhead stretch by keeping the elbows bent as the hands pass up the center of the body. When the arms pass head level, they start to straighten and the hands are grabbed in the entry position (see Figure 4.20, a-d).

2. Pike-out.

The diver extends the legs at the knee joint while remaining in a pike position at the hips. As the legs straighten at the knees, the arms move from their spinning position to a lateral shoulder-level location. Following this preliminary move to an open-pike position, the diver then straightens at the hips while the arms move laterally to the overhead stretch (see Figure 4.21, a-d).

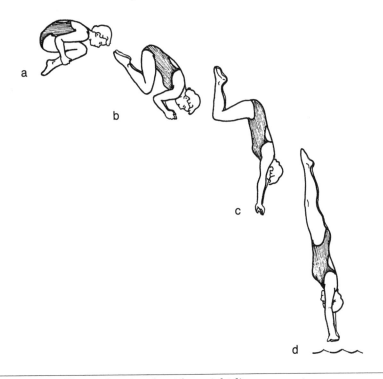

Figure 4.20 Forward/Inward optionals with straight-line come-out.

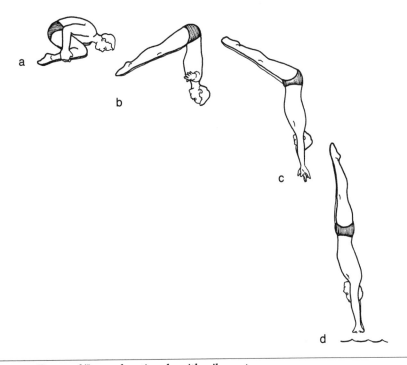

Figure 4.21 Forward/Inward optionals with pike-out.

Divers use the straight-line kick when there is not a lot of time to prepare for the entry, because this kick takes much less time to perform than the pike-out method of come-out. Divers usually prefer the pike-out when enough time is available to use this technique, because it gives the diver more time to see the entry point and more opportunity to adjust the entry when the body is straightened and the arms brought overhead.

Backward and reverse somersaulting dives in tuck and pike position also have two methods of come-out.

Method	Description
1. Straight line.	This is the same as the method used for forward and inward somersaulting dives, only it is done in the backward direction. The diver extends the legs in line with the upper body as the arms move to an overhead stretch. The head moves from its slightly forward position in the somersault to a neutral position as the stretch takes place (see Figure 4.22, a-d).

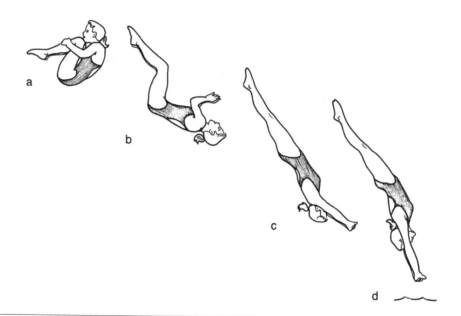

Figure 4.22   Backward/Reverse optionals with straight-line come-out.

Method	Description
2. Grab and stretch.	In tuck spinning dives, the diver extends the legs at the knees while maintaining a slight pike at the hip joint. In pike spinning dives, the body opens at the hip joint and maintains the same slight pike. In either case, as the opening takes place, the hands are grabbed in the entry position and are held momentarily in place somewhere between the lower abdominal area and the middle of the chest, depending on the diver's preference. The head stays tilted slightly forward toward the chest as the kick and grab motions occur. The diver then brings the arms up the midline of the body and to the

overhead stretching position. As the arms move up the body, the diver moves from the slight pike position to a slight arch. As the hands pass head level, the head moves from its forward position to a neutral alignment with the body, with the eyes looking back toward the water (see Figure 4.23, a-d).

Figure 4.23   Backward/Reverse optionals with grab-and-stretch come-out.

Divers use the straight-line come-out when there is not much time to prepare for the entry, whereas the grab-and-stretch method is utilized when time permits. The diver can more easily avoid developing an overly arched body position during entry with the grab-and-stretch technique because there is more time to develop a firm body position before the stretch begins.

Forward Come-Outs

From the 3-meter board, the diver sits forward in a tuck position at the end of the board and rolls forward into a dive. While leaving the board, the diver does a lineup using either the straight-line (see Figure 4.24, a-e) or pike-out (see Figure 4.25, a-d) method of come-out. The diver can do the same drill in the closed pike position.

On the 1-meter board, the diver can perform a forward dive tuck either from the standing position or with an approach, to practice both come-out methods and the entry. The forward dive is usually not performed in closed-pike position, because this tends to cause the diver to overrotate and not effectively practice a correct entry.

Figure 4.24 Forward tuck roll-off from 3-meter height, with straight-line come-out.

Figure 4.25 Forward tuck roll-off from 3-meter height, with pike-out.

Inward Come-Outs

Either from the 1- or 3-meter board, the diver practices an inward dive tuck using the two come-out methods. Again, an inward dive closed pike should not be done, because of control problems.

Backward Come-Outs

Tuck and pike roll-offs from the 3-meter board are good ways to practice the two backward somersaulting come-out actions (see Figure 4.26, a-e, and Figure 4.27, a-d). Because the roll-off method has been previously described, it need not be explained again. The diver can also practice come-out techniques for tuck spinning dives from the 1-meter board while doing a backward dive tuck.

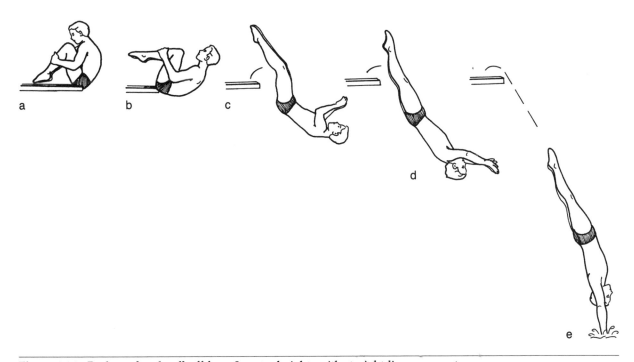

Figure 4.26 Backward tuck roll-off from 3-meter height, with straight-line come-out.

The diver can practice the pike grab-and-stretch come-out actions while doing a backward dive pike, with some variations from the usual mechanics. As the diver takes off, the jump and reach are the same as for a normal back dive pike; however, as the dive rises and the pike position takes place, the diver clasps the hands together and places them in front of the abdomen. At the peak of the dive, the body begins to extend to a straight position, and the diver performs the grab-and-stretch come-out actions (see Figure 4.28, a-f). As in all the other backward and reverse lineups, the diver holds the head in a slightly forward tilted position as the opening occurs and then moves it to a neutral position as the entry stretch begins; the eyes look back toward the water.

Reverse Come-Outs

The reverse dive tuck, which the diver does either standing or with an approach from the 1-meter board, affords the best method of practicing the tuck somersault come-outs. As for the backward lineups, the diver uses the same type of modified reverse dive pike to practice the pike somersault come-out movements.

Figure 4.27 Backward pike roll-off from 3-meter height, with grab-and-stretch come-out.

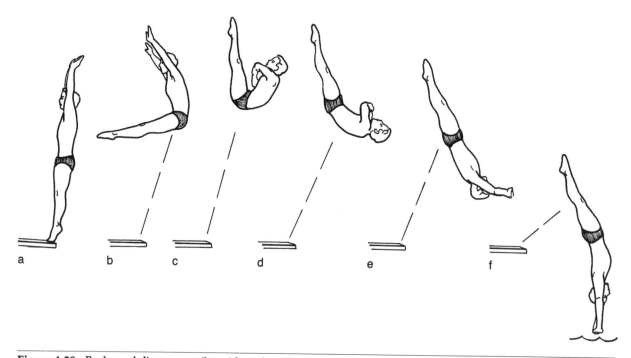

Figure 4.28 Backward dive open pike with grab-and-stretch come-out.

SUMMARY

There are many ways to practice entries and the various types of movements needed for different types of dives. If the diver practiced all of these drills, the time consumed would be inordinate. The diver should first learn all the methods described here, and then you should choose the drills that produce the best results and those that best fit the diver's needs. These needs may change as dives are eliminated from and added to the diver's list of dives, so the entry drills that the diver practices should be adjusted accordingly. The more proficient a diver becomes at come-outs, lineups, and entries as practiced in these drills, the more easily he or she will be able to finish the basic and optional dives with control and accuracy.

5
CHAPTER

SOMERSAULTING DIVES

Somersaulting dives are performed in four directions: forward, backward, reverse, and inward. Because the methods of initiating rotation in the forward and inward dives are similar, and the rotation methods are also similar between the backward and reverse spinning dives, this is the order of presentation. However, all of the dives differ in the point where balance is maintained and the way the takeoffs are performed, due to the way the forces involved in creating the rotation affect the distance from the board. The forward flying somersault dives are also presented as part of the forward, inward somersault section.

FORWARD SOMERSAULTING DIVES

When the diver lands on the board out of the hurdle, he or she should maintain the center of balance over the front of the feet. The sequence of arm and body motions used to depress the springboard are the same as described in the section concerning boardwork. The arms should swing up to a position overhead so they are in line with the head and upper body. Even though most divers have some elbow bend during the upswing of the arms in the press, the arms should return to a straight and elbow-locked position when they reach the overhead position. At this point, a diver may deliberately bend (cock) the elbows with the hands located behind the head in order to snap the arms from this bent position to a straight position and develop more arm speed and transfer of momentum to the rotational force. This aid to rotation, however, is not aesthetically pleasing and should be avoided.

As the arms complete their upswing, the diver must shift the center of balance forward when the board begins its upward thrust and just before the rotational forces are initiated. If the diver's weight moves forward before the arms swing up and before the board begins its upward movement, the diver will be out of balance and the dive will move too far from the board. Conversely, if the weight is located too far back at this point, the dive will be too close to the board and will spin slower, because the board will not aid rotation as much. The degree of forward lean occurring at this point directly relates to the number of somersaults to be performed. There are two reasons for this:

1. The more forward the angle of the body as the board gives its thrust, the greater the rotational force imparted to the diver. However, this lean also causes the board to push the diver out from the board on takeoff.
2. The more somersaults performed, the more rotational force needed. The greater the rotational force generated, the more the diver will travel backward into the board (review Figure 3.3).

In order to gain maximum efficiency of takeoff and somersault momentum, the diver must develop enough forward lean so that the thrust of the board pushing the diver out and the amount of movement back toward the board from the rotational force result in the desired angle of takeoff and correct distance from the board.

Because the greater the number of somersaults performed means the greater force required, resulting in the diver traveling backward into the board more, greater forward lean can occur with a resultant correct flight path.

The diver develops forward somersault rotation in a *one-piece movement* of the arms (held straight and parallel), head, and torso into a piking movement as the legs extend from the board and the board propels the diver upward. The position of the upper body and legs prior to the somersaulting motion is constant for all dives; however, the greater the number of somersaults being done, the greater the amount of piking motion needed before the feet leave the board. Note the differences in trunk positions during takeoff in Figure 5.1, a-c, for forward 1-1/2, 2-1/2, and 3-1/2 somersaults in the pike position.

a   b   c

Figure 5.1 Comparison of takeoff positions for the forward 1-1/2 somersault (a), the forward 2-1/2 somersault (b), and the forward 3-1/2 somersault (c).

In order for the diver to initiate spin effectively, this one-piece action is necessary. If the head drops before the arms and torso or the arms move down before the head and body, the diver will lose rotation. Also, the upper body must remain in alignment as the piking action occurs. If the chest area changes to a concave or convex shape and the back becomes either very hunched or arched, the diver will lose spinning force. Just as the feet leave the board, the arms move down in front of the body and reach for the tuck or pike position.

Figure 5.2, a-d, illustrates the correct technique of beginning forward rotation. Note that from the hips to the fingertips, the body moves as one unit in the beginning of the somersaulting motion.

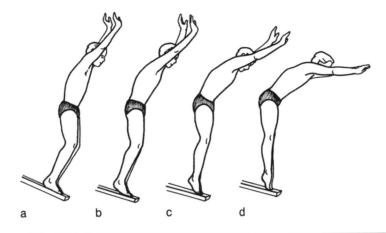

Figure 5.2 Forward/Inward one-piece movement.

INWARD SOMERSAULTING DIVES

The method of creating rotation is the same for inward somersaulting dives as for forward spins. The one-piece movement of the arms, head, and upper body, timed with the extension of the legs and the upward thrust of the board, is essential.

The key to performing good inward optionals lies in how the diver maintains balance during the press and initiation of the somersault. Because developing the rotation causes the board to push the diver away on takeoff (review Figure 3.4), any lean or movement of the balance backward prior to the somersaulting action will cause the diver to be too far from the board. A loss of balance backward also prevents the thrust of the board from aiding the diver into the rotation and inhibits the diver's ability to get full extension from the legs and ankles. Throughout the press until the start of the piking motion to initiate spin, it is crucial that the diver keep the balance absolutely steady. Balance should not shift either forward or backward.

Notice in Figure 5.3, a and b, the comparison of balance and takeoff position between the inward 1-1/2-somersault dive in tuck position and the inward 2-1/2-somersault dive in pike position.

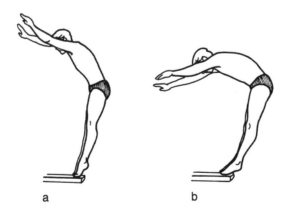

Figure 5.3 Comparison of the inward 1-1/2 somersault in pike position (a) and the inward 2-1/2 somersault in pike position (b).

The Right Feeling

When the diver correctly executes forward and inward somersaults, he or she feels as though the motion is in an upward and forward direction. There should be little sensation of a downward throw. If the diver does feel like the somersaulting motion is down, the movements to create spin are occurring too early and before the "kick" of the springboard. In performing the forward and inward somersault takeoff, the diver should feel like he or she is rolling over a barrel before moving to the tuck or pike position.

Visual Cues

Some visual cues will help to ensure that the diver makes the correct movements at the right time. As the diver presses the board and begins the somersaulting action in the forward or inward takeoff, the head should remain level. The eyes should focus on the far side of the pool for the front takeoff and either on the back end of the board or on the wall behind the board for inward takeoffs. After initiating the one-piece movement, the diver should look at the legs, just as they come off the board. These visual cues will help the diver keep the head up in position during the throwing motion while getting the proper timing of the rotational force; the cues will also ensure that the head and body move down into the somersault action at the correct moment. These visual cues are illustrated in Figure 5.4, a and b.

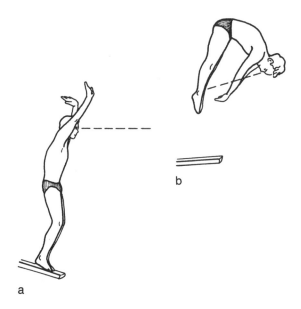

Figure 5.4   Visual cues for forward/inward optional takeoffs.

Getting Into Position

Just as the feet leave the board, the arms move down in front of the body to assume either the tuck or pike position. In the tuck position, the diver draws the thighs to the chest while the hands grasp the shins midway between the knee and ankle and pull the heels to the buttocks. The head should be positioned with the chin in tight and tilted down so the line of sight is over the top of the knees. If the diver pulls the head down too far so he or she is looking through the upper thigh area, this will affect spatial orientation and impair the diver's ability to sight the entry point and complete the dive vertically. The diver will also have a strong tendency to overrotate. No matter where the head is positioned, the diver must keep the eyes open throughout the spin.

The diver can best accomplish the pike position by moving the arms so the elbows are at the knees while the arms are straight and the hands are well past the legs (see Figure 5.5, a-d). At this point the arms wrap around the backs of the knees so the forearms hold the legs with each hand touching the outside of the opposite leg and each palm facing forward.

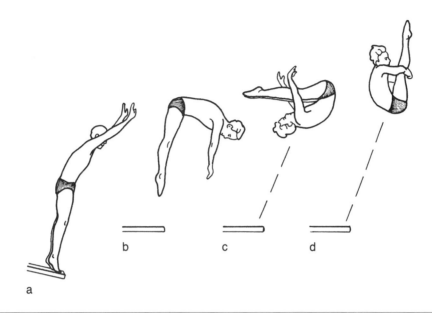

Figure 5.5 Forward/Inward pike position.

This method of assuming the pike allows the diver to quickly achieve a very compact position, resulting in greater acceleration. The alternate technique is for the diver to grasp the backs of the knees with the hands and then to begin pulling into a tight position. Although many divers use this, it is not as effective for multiple somersault dives.

When in the pike, the diver can use one of two techniques of head position and line of sight. The diver can lay the face directly into the legs so the eyes sight between the lower legs; this orients the diver and allows him or her to see the entry point. This produces a tighter and therefore a faster spin. However, if the diver has trouble with being spatially aware of position or cannot see well this way, he or she can tilt the chin upward slightly so the eyes look up and sight over the toes.

Coming Out

Regardless of whether the diver is in tuck or pike position, he or she will complete headfirst-entry somersaulting dives using one of the two somersault come-out techniques discussed in chapter 4. If there is adequate time, the diver should use the pike-out method (see Figure 5.6, a-f); if there is little time to complete the dive, the diver should use the straight-line kick-out (see Figure 5.7, a-f). In feetfirst entries, the body moves from the tuck or pike position directly to a straight line with the arms at the sides, palms on the side of the upper leg, and toes pointed. Throughout this opening, the head remains still. Obviously, the diver will have to learn from repetition at what point in the spin to start the opening. As a general rule for the headfirst-entry dives in the tuck position, the kick-out begins as the diver's head passes through the vertical position in the last rotation of the dive (see Figure 5.8, e and f); for the pike position, the opening occurs at the 1/4-somersault position in the last somersault of rotation (see Figure 5.9f).

Study the forward and inward somersaulting dives in Figures 5.6 through 5.13 to get a visual picture of the correct takeoff, somersault position, and come-out technique for these types of dives.

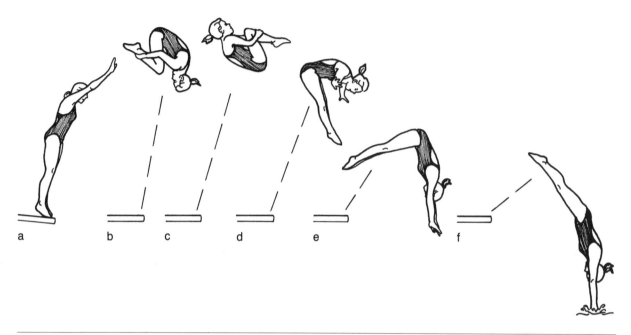

Figure 5.6 Forward 1-1/2 somersault in tuck position with pike-out from 1-meter height.

Figure 5.7 Forward 1-1/2 somersault in pike position with straight come-out from 1-meter height.

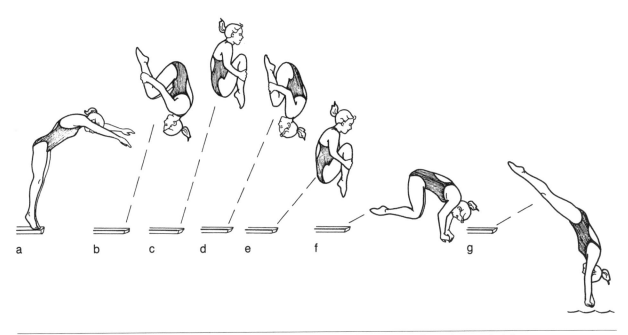

Figure 5.8 Forward 2-1/2 somersault in tuck position with straight come-out from 1-meter height.

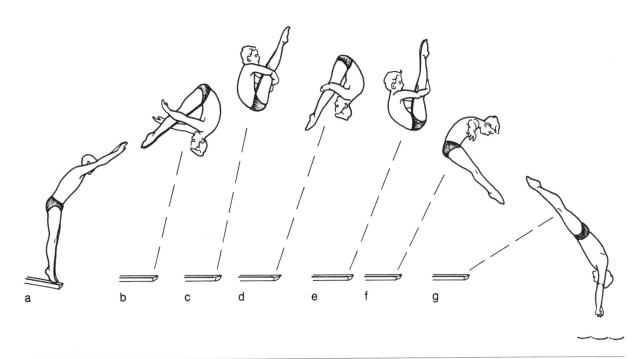

Figure 5.9 Forward 2-1/2 somersault in pike position with pike-out from 1-meter height.

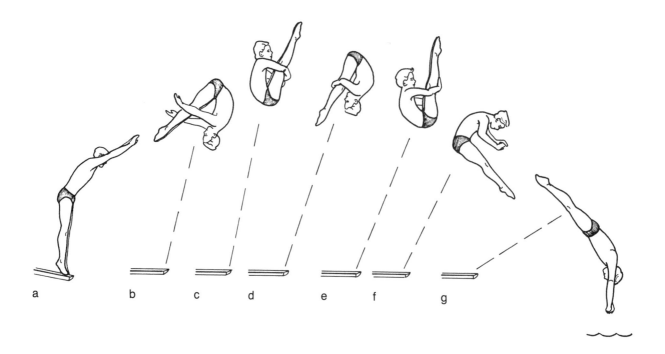

Figure 5.10 Forward 2-1/2 somersault in pike position with straight come-out, from 1-meter height.

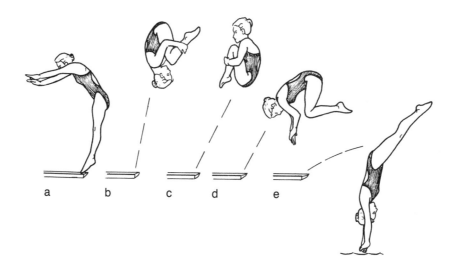

Figure 5.11 Inward 1-1/2 somersault in tuck position with straight come-out, from 1-meter height.

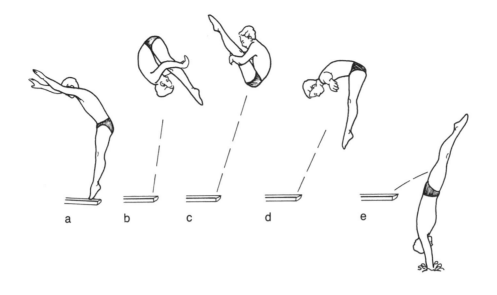

Figure 5.12 Inward 1-1/2 somersault in pike position with pike-out from 1-meter height.

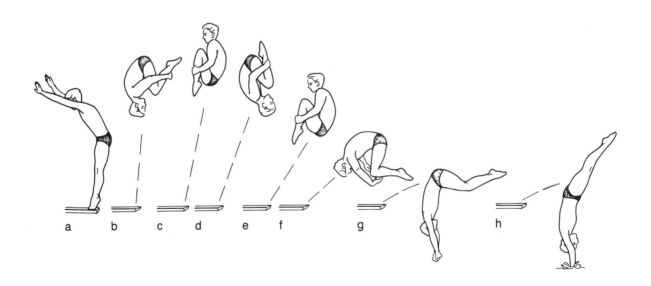

Figure 5.13 Inward 2-1/2 somersault in tuck position with straight come-out from 1-meter height.

FLYING SOMERSAULT DIVES

The flying forward and inward somersault dives start like strong forward or inward dives in the straight position. The arms are straight and parallel overhead at takeoff, and the head is in a neutral position with the eyes looking at the other side of the pool. The diver needs more pike at the hips, however, than in the straight dives, in order to create more rotation from the board. As soon as the feet leave the board, the arms move laterally to shoulder level, while the body moves from pike to straight as soon as possible. This position is held until a 1/2-somersault point, when the diver moves to a tuck or pike position to complete the desired amount of rotation. During the rotation from takeoff to the 1/2 somersault, the diver gradually shifts the focus of the eyes from the far side of the pool to the entry point, in order to keep the head up in a neutral position. In the tuck position the hands grab the legs at midshin level, but in the pike dives the diver can use either a closed- or open-pike position.

If only one somersault is being performed, the diver straightens the body for the entry with the arms at the sides. For 1-1/2- or 2-1/2-somersault dives, the come-out is the same as for the other forward and inward somersault optionals: either the straight-line or the open-pike come-out.

Flying inward somersault dives are rarely performed, due to the difficulty of holding the straight position to the 1/2-somersault point. Forward flying 2-1/2-somersault dives are also seldom done in competition. Therefore, only the forward flying 1-1/2 somersault from a closed, pike position is illustrated in Figure 5.14, a-f.

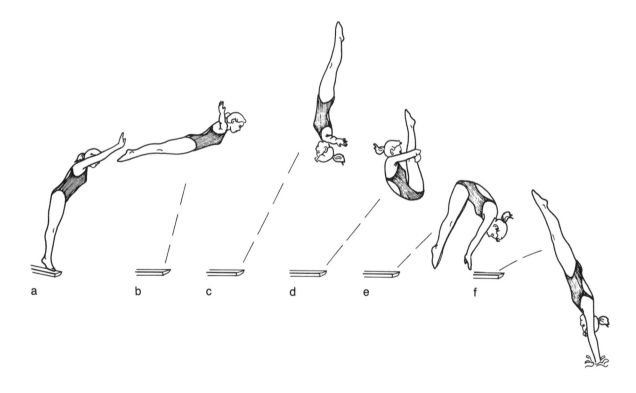

a   b   c   d   e   f

Figure 5.14   Forward flying 1-1/2 somersault in closed-pike position, from 1-meter height.

BACKWARD SOMERSAULTING DIVES

For safety's sake the coach and diver should have a thorough understanding of the forces involved in backward somersaulting dives. This will ensure correct distance from the board during the learning process.

The Takeoff

By reviewing Figure 3.6 you will see that the action of creating backward rotation causes the diver to travel forward toward the board. As the force generated to create spin increases, the force pushing the diver into the board increases.

To compensate for this situation, the diver needs to shift the balance backward through the hips as he or she moves through the bottom of the back press and as the arms swing upward. This change in balance must not occur at the top of the press, with the upper body, because the amount of lean will be excessive. A lack of control will result, and the dive will finish too far away from the board, with insufficient lift.

The amount of backward lean or "sitting away from the board" must be such that the outward thrust of the board caused by this balance and the inward force of the somersault action result in the correct angle of the takeoff and line of flight for the dive (see Figure 5.15, a-c).

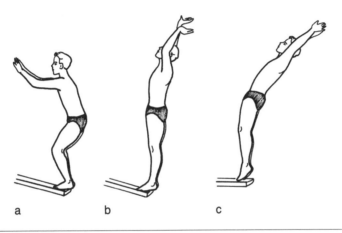

a   b   c

Figure 5.15 Backward lean with forward hip thrust.

As this positioning of the center of balance takes place, the arms continue their swinging motion up in front of the body; as the arms pass above head level, the body begins to extend. As the body nears full extension and the arms are directly overhead, the diver initiates somersault rotation by a combination of two motions: lifting the hips up and forward while continuing to push against the board with the legs, and hyperextending the torso backward as the arms continue to reach upward and backward over the head. The diver must keep the arms as straight as possible and parallel through these movements and must initiate the arching motion from the hip joint; the diver must not allow the upper body alignment to break down so the arch is primarily in the upper back and chest area. Some elbow bend may occur approximately halfway through the upswing (normal for most divers, although a few can keep the elbows straight), but the arms should definitely be straight as they pass above head level. The head should remain in a neutral position throughout the press and should be located between the arms at the point of takeoff; the eyes should look straight ahead but not focus on any particular point.

The body shape created by these movements simulates a shallow "C" or arc-shaped position. This description can give the diver a visual picture of the correct takeoff position. Figure 5.16 shows this position.

Figure 5.16   Backward takeoff in C position.

Tuck and Pike Positions

In tuck and pike somersaulting dives, as soon as the diver's feet leave the board, the diver accelerates rotation by closing the body from the extended position to the spinning position in one of two ways.

- Direct closure
- Circular closure

The diver executes direct closure by bringing the arms down in front of the body while lifting the legs either to the tuck or pike position. The diver keeps the arms straight during the beginning of this motion. As the arms approach the legs, the elbows are bent and the hands grasp the legs at the midpoint of the shins for the tuck; the arms wrap around the legs at knee level for the pike (similar to the forward somersaulting dives). As these movements take place, the head and upper body should move forward toward the legs to assist in speeding up the closing time and thus accelerate the rotation quickly. It is very important that the head does not tilt backward during closure, regardless of which method the diver uses. A visual cue to help prevent this backward tilting is for the diver to keep the line of sight directed so he or she can see the knees coming into the tuck position (see Figure 5.17, a-f), or the legs and feet moving into the pike position (see Figure 5.18, a-e). This visual contact should occur as early during closure as possible.

a   b   c   d   e   f

Figure 5.17   Backward somersault in tuck position with direct closure.

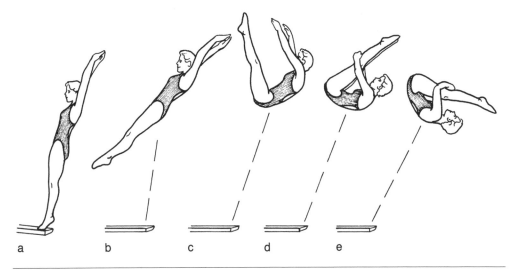

Figure 5.18   Backward somersault in pike position with direct closure.

Circular closure starts from the same takeoff position as direct closure. Instead of moving in front of the body, the arms follow a backward and downward circling pattern while the legs are lifted to the tuck or pike position and the head and upper body push toward the legs to assist the rapid closure movement.

The path of the arms should be lateral and slightly behind the body line. For the tuck, the hands should move down as far as the hips before grabbing the legs; for the pike, the hands should move past the hips and legs, before the arms wrap around the legs. As an aid to making the circle motion easier and faster, the diver can turn the hand and arm as the movement begins, so the little finger points in the direction of the circle (inward rotation of the shoulder joint). This eliminates friction in the shoulder area. Throughout this movement, the diver should keep the arms straight until they must bend to catch the legs. An important concept to understand here is that as the arms circle, the legs move into the upper body before any contact between arms and legs occurs. The grabbing motion in the tuck is done from in front of the shins into the body, and the wraparound in the pike is from behind the legs into the body. In other words, the diver assumes the tuck or pike position as tightly as possible before the arms pull the position even tighter (see Figure 5.19, a-e, and Figure 5.20, a-f).

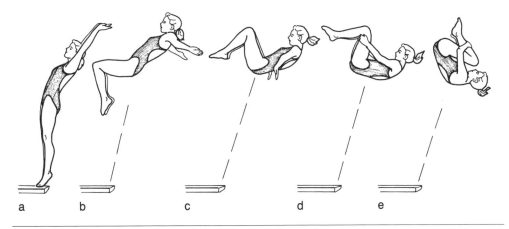

Figure 5.19   Circular closure for backward optional in tuck position.

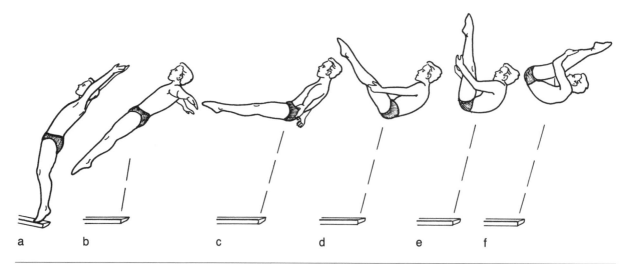

a   b   c   d   e   f

Figure 5.20   Circular closure for backward optional in pike position.

The diver should learn the direct closure method first. Practice should continue with this technique until the diver can take off with a straight and parallel overhead reach of the arms, combined with full body extension and control of balance. Establishing these fundamentals is essential before the diver learns the circular closure technique.

For most divers, the circular closure technique is more effective than the direct closure movement. When the diver uses the circular closure technique, the backward and downward action of the arms not only shortens the radius of rotation more quickly, but also assists the upper body in momentarily stopping rotation, resulting in a transfer of momentum to the legs and a corresponding increased speed of closure and a tighter tuck or pike position. When the legs catch up with the torso, the body begins rotating again as a unit.

REVERSE SOMERSAULTING DIVES

The diver develops rotation and moves to a tuck or pike position in reverse somersaulting dives in exactly the same way as for backward somersaulting dives with regard to movements and techniques. The major consideration is for the diver to create adequate rotation while assuring safe and proper distance from the springboard. The diver accomplishes this by attaining the correct balance in the press and by moving to the C body position for takeoff with the proper sequence of body movements.

The Takeoff

When dropping from the hurdle to the board, the diver should keep the balance slightly backward (this differs from the forward takeoff, in which the balance is over the front of the feet). Because the forces generated in creating the rotation push the diver away from the board (review Figure 3.7), no forward lean is needed to achieve good distance. While the diver depresses the board and swings the arms up to the preliminary takeoff position, no change in balance should occur. After the diver reaches the preliminary takeoff position, the body should move into the C position as described for backward somersaulting takeoffs. It is crucial at this point that the diver move the balance forward by keeping the shoulders in one place, while the legs drive the hips upward and forward. Because the direction of takeoff for reverse somersaults is opposite that for backward somersault, the body is in a reverse C position, as shown in Figure 5.21. If the diver reaches this position by keeping the hips in one location while moving the upper body and shoulders backward, the center of balance will not travel away from the board as rotation is developed, and the diver will strike the board.

Figure 5.21   Reverse takeoff in C position.

To reach the C position correctly, the diver can imagine a 10-meter platform directly across the pool from the springboard; the diver should try to push the hips up and forward toward the edge of the platform.

Head Position

As with the forward somersaulting dives, head position in the backward and reverse somersaulting dives is crucial. In the tuck dives, the diver should draw the chin in tight to the chest and direct the line of sight over the top of the knees. The knees may be spread slightly to aid vision and increase the speed of rotation, but they should be kept inside shoulder-width and the feet should be together. If the diver sights down through the legs too far, disorientation and a tendency to overrotate the entry may result. Pike dives provide the same option as in the forward somersault dives. The diver can position the head so he or she can see through the lower legs (it helps to be slightly bowlegged), or if this is not effective, the diver can keep the chin up slightly and look over the toes.

BACKWARD AND REVERSE 1-1/2 SOMERSAULTS STRAIGHT

Backward and reverse somersaulting dives in the straight position involve the same balance and initiation of rotation techniques as in the tuck and pike positions. The difference occurs in the movements after the diver leaves the board. As soon as possible the diver brings the arms (which are kept straight and parallel) down in front of the body, while the head tilts back, the eyes look back, and the upper body continues to pull in the rotating direction. When the arms approach the body, the diver uses one of the following positions.

1. The diver brings the hands together, bends the elbows, and places the palms on the abdominal area somewhere between the chest and the hips, depending on diver preference.
2. The diver keeps the arms straight and places the hands on the front of the thighs.

Regardless of the arm position, the arms remain still until the stretch for the entry.

COMING OUT

The diver comes out of backward and reverse tuck and pike somersaulting rotations by using one of the two methods described in chapter 4: the straight-line come-out, or grab-and-stretch actions. If there is little time to complete the dive, the diver should use the straight-line come-out. If there is time to perform the grab-and-stretch technique, this is preferred. Through repetition and experience the diver must learn when to begin the kick-out based on the speed of rotation and distance from the water. As a general rule, the come-out for tuck dives starts when the dive is approximately at 3/4 to 7/8 somersault for 1-1/2-rotation dives (see Figure 5.22d), 1-3/4 to 1-7/8 for 2-1/2-rotation dives, and 2-3/4 to 2-7/8 for 3-1/2-rotation dives. In pike dives, the come-out begins at the 1-1/8- to 1-1/4- (see Figure 5.23d), 2-1/8- to 2-1/4-, and 3-1/8- to 3-1/4-somersault positions for 1-1/2-, 2-1/2-, and 3-1/2-rotation dives, respectively.

The diver can complete the backward and reverse 1-1/2 somersault in straight position with the grab-and-stretch technique (see Figure 5.24e), or by straightening the arms and moving them in a lateral path (see Figure 5.28e) to the overhead entry stretch position.

No matter what body position the diver uses, the grab-and-stretch come-out method affords the diver greater control of rotation in dives that are completed easily and thus have a tendency to cause the diver to overrotate. The more control or "checking" of the rotation is needed, the farther the arms extend away from the body as they move overhead for the entry. The outward and backward movement of the arms causes a temporary reaction movement of the legs in the opposite direction of rotation. In dives that spin very fast, the arms may move from the grab position to the entry while remaining completely straight. Only acute awareness of rotational speed and of time remaining before the entry will tell the diver how much to straighten the arms during the movement to the entry stretch position. Experimentation and experience are the keys.

Analyze the illustrations in Figures 5.22 through 5.28 to get a visual picture of how the backward and reverse somersaulting dives are performed.

a   b   c   d   e   f

Figure 5.22 Backward 1-1/2 somersault in tuck position with direct closure and straight come-out, from 1-meter height.

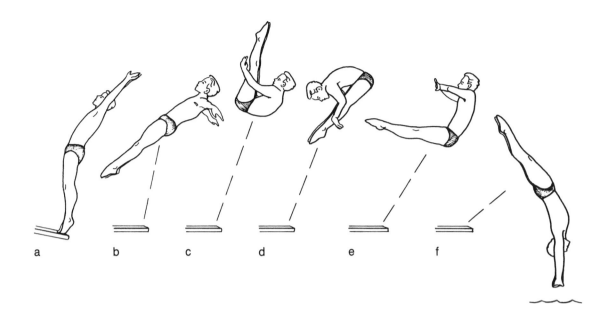

Figure 5.23 Backward 1-1/2 somersault in pike position with circular closure and grab-and-stretch come-out from 1-meter height.

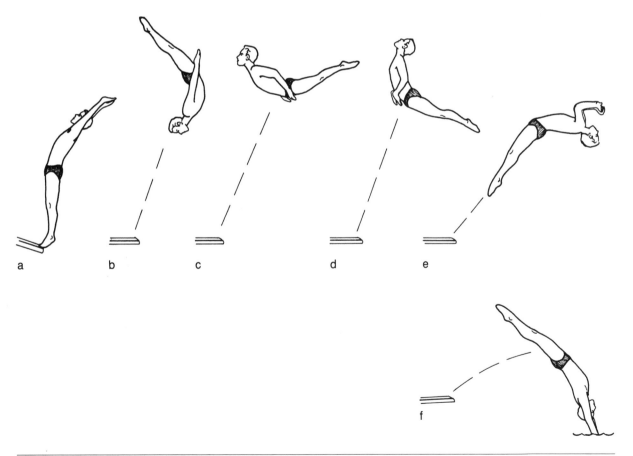

Figure 5.24 Backward 1-1/2 somersault in straight position from 1-meter height.

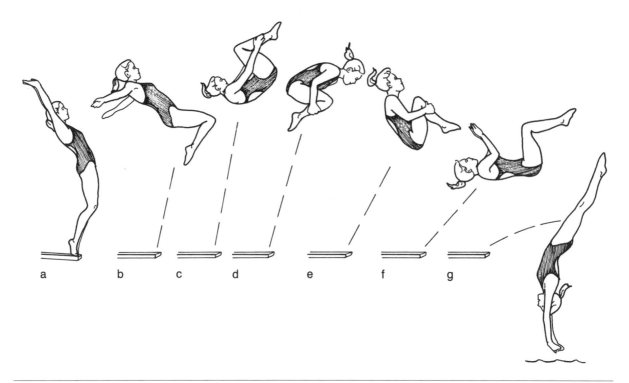

Figure 5.25   Reverse 1-1/2 somersault in tuck position with circular closure and straight come-out from 1-meter height.

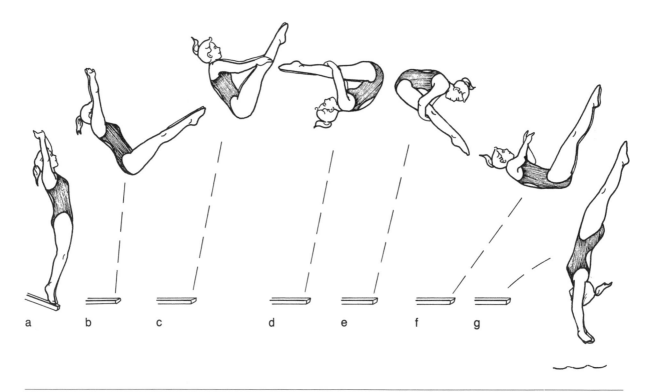

Figure 5.26   Reverse 1-1/2 somersault in pike position with straight come-out from 1-meter height.

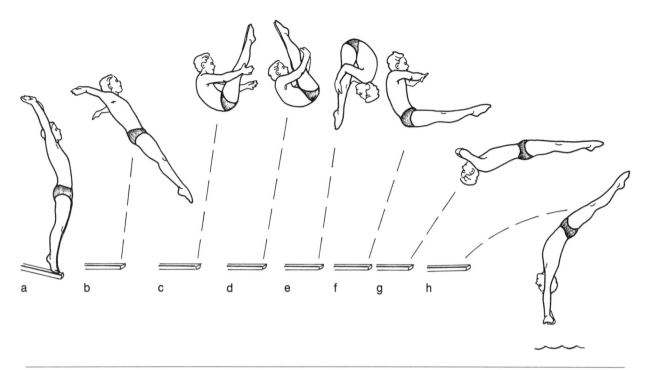

Figure 5.27 Reverse 1-1/2 somersault in pike position with circle closure and grab-and-stretch come-out from 1-meter height.

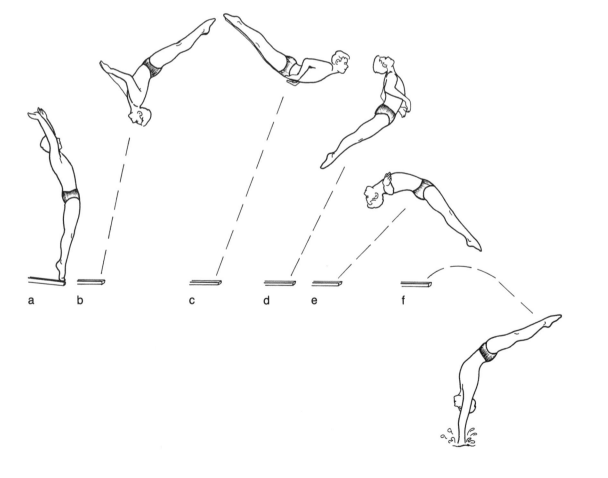

Figure 5.28 Reverse 1-1/2 somersault in straight position with lateral come-out from 3-meter height.

VISUAL SPOTTING

For many years divers have used a technique called *spotting* to assist in spatial orientation and knowing when to come out of the somersaulting dives. Spotting entails visually sighting a particular point on each somersault rotation. It is similar to the way ballet dancers fix their vision on one point and quickly return to look at the point during each rotation in a series of rotations. Dancers, however, perform rotations on a different axis than divers and have the luxury of greater head movement to accomplish this feat. Divers can use spotting on forward and inward as well as backward and reverse somersaulting dives. However, the practice is much more prevalent in the backward and reverse somersault dives, because these dives usually pose more difficulties for the diver, as far as knowing when to come out of the spin.

Backward and Reverse Spotting

During backward and reverse spinning dives with headfirst entries, visual spotting occurs at the 3/4- to 7/8-somersault point for each rotation to be completed in tuck spins, and at the 1-1/8- to 1-1/4-somersault point for pike dives. Thus, the diver will spot once at this point for a 1-1/2-somersault dive, twice for a 2-1/2-somersault dive, and three times for a 3-1/2-somersault dive. In backward somersaulting dives, the diver may spot the front few feet of the springboard or the water below, depending on the number of somersaults being done and the diver's preference. In 1-1/2-somersault dives, the board is almost always the spot point. In 2-1/2- and 3-1/2-somersault dives, either spot is used. If the dive is easy to complete and tends to cause overrotation, spotting the water is best, because the diver sees the water sooner than the springboard and will be able to kick out sooner. In dives that the diver doesn't have as much time to complete, spotting the board causes the diver to kick the legs closer to vertical.

Divers spot reverse somersault dives by looking at the water. The exact point on the water that the diver sights depends on how much time is available to complete the dive. For a dive high off the water, the spot needs to be directly under the diver in the entry area, whereas a dive that finishes lower would be spotted farther out toward the middle of the pool.

When the diver sees the designated spot, he or she should initiate the kick-out, using whatever method the diver chooses. The diver must keep in mind, however, that spotting is not a panacea. It does not guarantee that the dive will finish correctly. Spotting is a visual cue that keeps the diver from coming out of the spin in a totally incorrect place. When the diver sees the spot and performs the kick-out, he or she must still be aware of how fast the somersault is rotating and how much time is available to complete the dive, and must kick the legs at an appropriate angle accordingly.

Most divers do not spot for forward and inward somersault dives. Because divers can usually feel and see their positions better on these dives, they do not need as much help with spatial orientation. Divers who do not possess this natural feeling and therefore have difficulty hitting these dives should use the spotting technique. The spotting method used for forward and inward somersault dives in tuck position differs somewhat from that for the forward and inward somersault dives in pike position. It is used only in headfirst entry dives of 2-1/2 or more rotations.

In pike dives, the spot is the water in front of the entry, and it is sighted between the 1/8- and 3/8-somersault position on each rotation, depending on the diver's head position. If the diver looks through the legs during the spin, he or she will see the spot between the 1/8- and 1/4-somersault rotation point each time around. If the diver keeps the chin up and the line of sight over the toes, he or she will see the spot between the 1/4- and 3/8-somersault point. Upon seeing the spot, the diver begins the kick-out according to how much time is left to complete the dive.

Tuck dives are spotted between the vertical head position at the completion of each rotation and the 1/8-somersault position. These dives present a different situation than the pike dives, because for tuck dives the legs are behind the head when spotting occurs, rather than in front of the head. If the dive spins very slow or finishes very close to the water, the diver can spot the water and begin the kick-out action just as in the pike position. However, if there is considerable time to complete the dive, and the diver spots the water and begins the come-out, the dive will overrotate. In these situations the diver must estimate when the spot will occur based on the spots in the previous somersaults and must begin the kick-out just as the spot comes into view, instead of when it is already in view.

Dry-Land Training for Learning Visual Spotting

The best way to learn the spotting techniques just discussed is on a trampoline or dry-land diving board with overhead safety equipment. In this situation the diver can totally concentrate on seeing the spots while you safely hold up and let down the diver. In addition, you can place a colorful towel in the location of the spot to aid the diver in seeing this area of each rotation. It is also helpful if you call "look" at the precise moment the diver should see the spot (or towel) on each revolution; this gives the diver a sense of timing. When spotting becomes consistent, eliminate the towel and verbal assistance.

Keeping the head position neutral and level and ensuring that the eyes look straight out of the eye socket are necessary to good spotting. If the head tilts back through the spin or drops very low, the diver will see the spot either early or late, respectively (or may not see the spot at all). If the eyes look up through the eyebrows or down through the lower eyelid, spotting is very difficult.

On backward and reverse somersault dives, sometimes a diver can look at and pass the first spot and then tilt the head back to see the next spot earlier and watch this spot longer, as the chin comes back in to a neutral position. The diver uses the same head movement on each rotation. This allows great visual and spatial orientation; however, the head motion does tend to slow the spin when the head tilts back in each revolution, so the diver must have plenty of time to complete the dive in order to use this technique.

In-Pool Training for Visual Spotting

Once the diver perfects spotting in the dry-land setting, it should be used in the pool. At first, the same aids used in the dry-land setting can be helpful in the pool. For backward and inward somersault dives, you can drape a colorful towel over the board just in front of the diver's feet to direct visual attention to that area during the dive. Even though the spot will not be quite where it should for the inward somersault dives, the towel can give the diver a clue as to when the spot should come into view.

For the forward and reverse somersaulting dives, it is more difficult to provide a colorful object for the diver to see while spinning, but this can be overcome. Almost all pools have the shepherd's crook and ring buoy lifesaving equipment. Tie the ring buoy to the crooked end of the pole and place a colorful towel over the top. Push the ring buoy out into the water, in line with the board and obviously far enough away so there is no danger of the diver landing on it. When the diver uses the 3-meter board, which is farther from the edge of the pool, arrange the same setup and use a second shepherd's crook to give more length to the pole; simply hook the crook under and over the last couple of feet of the first pole, or tie the poles together.

As with the dry-land training, it's worthwhile for you to give verbal cues as to when the diver should look for the spot in each somersault. As the diver becomes proficient at seeing the spots consistently, discontinue the aids.

CALLING DIVERS OUT

Many divers who are learning a new somersault dive or practicing one they haven't performed for a long time like to have a coach's verbal command to cue them when to kick out. This method is termed "calling the diver out." This is a big responsibility for you and a great indication of the diver's confidence in your ability. Obviously, neither you nor the diver wants the call to be given at the wrong time, so you need some guidelines to follow in these situations.

You must thoroughly understand the visual spotting section just presented. For any particular dive, you should give the call as the diver's head enters the spotting area. It doesn't matter if the diver is actually spotting or not. It *is* important that you can see where this area is, in the last somersault, and can react with a "hup" or "hut" command—and make it *loud*!

The best way to practice calling is to watch a diver in training and mentally call the diver out of a dive. Then determine if the call is correct by observing whether the diver kicks when you call and whether he or she hits the dive. For example, if the diver kicks before you call, and hits the dive, you are too late.

When you become proficient at calling when the diver's head is in the spotting area, you need to learn to adjust the call a little early or late if the speed of rotation is extremely fast or slow.

TRAINING FOR SOMERSAULTS

The most effective way for the diver to practice the fundamentals of somersaulting forward and backward is on a trampoline. The beginning diver should practice only with the aid of the overhead safety equipment. As the skill level increases so that the diver is in good control and has good spatial awareness, he or she can practice these basic single somersaults without the safety harness. If the diver is advanced enough, and you have adequate skill with the safety equipment, the diver can progress to training with double somersaults in the forward and backward directions.

The diver can also practice somersaults from the deck of the pool into the water. Depending on the distance from the water to the deck and on the strength and skill of the diver, the diver may use a low bench to make this training easier.

For very advanced divers, practicing somersaults on a mat or from a low bench to a mat is very productive. Such practice not only helps the diver groove the motions of the skill, but it also works on speed of execution and leg development due to the landing impact. It is important that the diver not overdo this type of training because of the possibility of leg injuries.

The diver can best accomplish the circular closure method of performing backward and reverse somersaults without the safety harness, because the ropes impede the circling motion. Practicing backward and reverse somersaults in the open-tuck and open-pike positions (no grabbing of the legs) on the trampoline, from the 1-meter board, and from the side of the pool gives the diver the best feel for how to do multiple somersaults with this technique. When the diver can correctly perform the single somersault action, he or she should try 1-1/2 and double somersaults from the 1-meter board. The open-tuck and open-pike somersault skills with circular closure are shown in Figures 5.29, a-f, and 5.30, a-f.

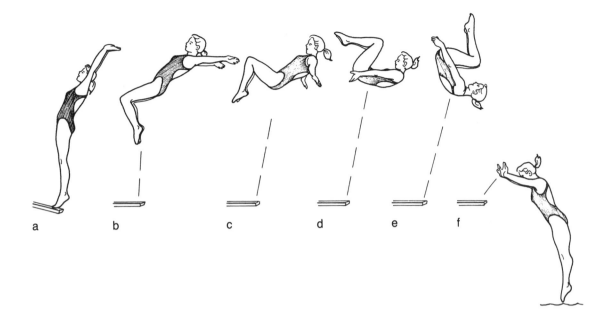

Figure 5.29 Circular closure in open-tuck position.

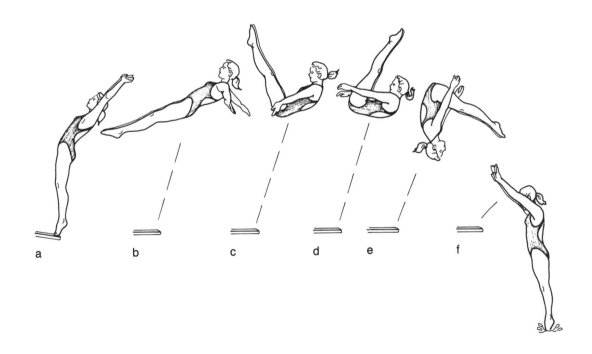

Figure 5.30 Circular closure in open-pike position.

SUMMARY

Throughout the diver's career, he or she must consistently work on the somersault actions to ensure a pattern of execution that can be repeated dive after dive. Even for the highly skilled world-class diver, this training should take place daily on the trampoline, dry-land diving board, tumbling mat, springboard, and platform, and from the side of the pool. The diver can vary when and how this practice occurs among these areas to relieve boredom of repetition.

6
CHAPTER

TWISTING DIVES

Twisting dives are the most complicated type of dives, because they involve two axes of rotation. When the diver combines somersaulting and twisting, more things can go wrong than when the diver is just somersaulting.

For you to successfully coach the twisting dives and for your diver to successfully perform these dives, you both need to know several things: the correct basic somersault skill for the type of twist performed, how and when the diver should initiate the twist, the relationship between speed of somersault and speed of twist for the various dives, the correct twisting position, and how the diver can stop the twist in preparation for the entry.

When the diver understands and learns these ingredients properly, twisting dives not only are easy but are the most enjoyable dives to perform. Divers with good basic twisting fundamentals rarely miss even the most difficult dives in this group.

THE MOST IMPORTANT FUNDAMENTAL

The most important fundamental to all twisting dives is that the diver establish somersault momentum on a straight axis of rotation and in line with the board. If the somersault is off line to one side or the other, it will be very difficult, if not impossible, for the diver to complete the twist correctly and perform a good finish of the dive. A diver who takes off to the side or off axis from the board on the basic somersault skill must correct this flaw before attempting to add any twists. Even a diver who can perform the basic somersault skills correctly may develop an off-axis somersault when learning the twisting part of the dive. This is usually caused by the diver starting the twist too early. To avoid this, you should do two things during the teaching process:

1. Constantly emphasize that the diver must develop the somersault momentum before he or she begins the twist.
2. Periodically check the straightness of the somersault axis from the front and rear views, even for the most advanced diver.

TYPES OF TWIST

There are two basic types of twisting dives: forward and backward. The movements of forward twisting can be used in forward and inward somersaulting dives, whereas backward twisting technique is used in backward and reverse somersaulting dives.

The major difference between the forward/inward and the backward/reverse twisting dives lies in the takeoff mechanics. For each group of dives (i.e., forward/inward and backward/reverse), the diver must follow the same principles of correct takeoff as described in the section concerning somersaulting optionals. Because inward twisting dives are rarely used, they are not included in this discussion.

FORWARD TWISTING DIVES

There are two different methods of learning the forward twisting dives. One method requires the diver to begin from an open-pike somersault; the other method utilizes a flying somersault starting technique. The diver should learn the open-pike forward somersault action first, and if this is not satisfactory, you can introduce the second method.

Before I describe these two twisting techniques, let's first discuss some general ideas and concepts about twisting that should help you and the diver understand and apply the specific information later.

Trampoline Versus Pool

The best and easiest place for the diver to learn all twisting skills is on a trampoline, with the aid of overhead spotting equipment. This situation gives you control of the diver and thus gives the diver complete freedom to concentrate on the movements. Using the trampoline and spotting equipment eliminates overriding concern about how the dive will finish. If the diver follows the principles and progressions presented here, learning should be safe and successful whether the diver attempts these skills on the trampoline or in the pool.

Basic Concepts

You and your diver must understand three basic concepts of forward twisting:

1. For the beginner, it is easiest to initiate the twisting movement in the second 1/2 of the somersault.
2. The twist begins simultaneously with the opening of the body from the pike to straight position.
3. The diver generates the twist by turning the upper body and moving the arms out and around the body.

Let's examine these three points in detail.

Twisting Late

Initiating the twist in the second 1/2 of the open-pike somersault (rather than in the middle) or in the first 1/2 of the somersault has several advantages.

- It ensures that the somersault is on the proper somersault axis before the diver starts the twist.

- By somersaulting before twisting, the diver increases significantly the opportunity to land safely on the feet.
- If the diver establishes somersault momentum first, he or she can develop twisting momentum easier.
- If the diver starts the twist at the point where he or she would normally come out of the open-pike somersault to land feetfirst on the water or trampoline, the diver doesn't have to think about moving the body from pike to straight. This will happen naturally, because the diver is used to opening at this point, and the force of gravity and the somersault momentum aid in the opening.

Simultaneous Twist and Opening

Many coaches and divers think the diver must open to a straight body line and then initiate the twist. This is not true! In fact, emphasizing a snap-out movement as a lead-up skill to twisting does two things:

1. It causes the diver to focus first on opening sharply from the pike, and then to focus on the twisting action, which gives the diver less time to concentrate on the twisting movements to be made. When the diver is somersaulting in an upside-down position and trying to twist for the first time, all focus needs to be on twisting.
2. The snapping motion from pike to straight can cause an arched body shape to develop, making twisting slow and much less efficient.

Initiating the Twist

A common misunderstanding about starting a twist is that moving the arms into a twisting placement position, tight to the body, develops the twist. Actually, moving the arms into the body accelerates the twist, but a turning motion of the upper body combined with movement of the arms in the direction of twist starts the twisting momentum. The diver should move the arms out and around the body first, and then, when the twist is moving, bring the arms into the body.

Open-Pike Twist Method

Twisting from the forward open pike somersault position is the most widely used technique for forward twisting dives. For most beginners it is also the easiest twisting method to learn.

Forward Somersault With 1 Twist

Before attempting this dive, the diver must determine in which direction the twist will take place. The diver can determine this by doing a front jump from the side of the pool and performing 1 twist, first in one direction and then in the other. Usually one direction feels better than the other and causes the twist to stay on a more vertical line. In the majority of cases, the diver does the twist in the opposite direction of the dominant arm: Right-handed people twist to the left, and vice versa.

With the direction of twist determined, the diver must learn to do a good forward somersault in the open-pike position (see Figure 6.1, a-e). The diver must perform this skill so that the rotation is completed easily and there is some drop from the end of the dive to the water. If this is not the case, the diver will not be able to complete the dive when the twist is introduced.

When the diver can achieve a good forward open-pike somersault, he or she can perform a single twist in the second 1/2 of the somersault. The diver should

Figure 6.1   Forward somersault in open-pike position.

first do an open-pike somersault and concentrate on what is visually prominent in the dive. Generally, a diver sees two things: the lower legs while the diver is in the pike position, and the water and other side of the pool when the diver comes out (or the area in front of the trampoline if the diver is in a spotting apparatus). Next the diver does an open-pike somersault, making sure he or she watches the lower legs until it's time to open for the entry or landing. Simultaneously with the opening of the body, the diver turns the upper body in the direction of the twist while moving the arms in the same direction, at chest level. The diver keeps the arms away from the body until the twist starts, then brings them into the body. Figure 6.2, a-d, shows the beginning of the twisting action from the open-pike position.

There are two accepted arm positions for twisting, regardless of whether the diver is performing forward or backward twisting dives. The first and easiest position to learn is the split arm method. Here, the diver places one arm across the chest (the right arm when the diver is twisting left and vice versa); the other arm is overhead, bent at a 90-degree angle so the bicep is against the ear and the forearm on top of the head. The second arm position is the arms-together technique; the hands are close together under the chin, the arms are bent, and the elbows are drawn close to the midline of the body. In either case, the diver must keep the elbows close to the body for a smooth and fast twist action. See Figure 6.3, a and b, for an illustration of these arm positions. After the body opens from pike to straight position, no arch or pike should be present and the head should be in a neutral position with the chin drawn in.

During the last 3/8 to 1/4 twist, the arms must begin to "square out" by moving away from the body in preparation for the entry or landing. If the diver is using the split arm position, the top arm moves first in an overhead direction, then upward, and then laterally down to shoulder level. When the top arm is approximately halfway to its lateral destination, the arm across the chest begins to move in a direct line to a straight and lateral location at shoulder height. Both arms

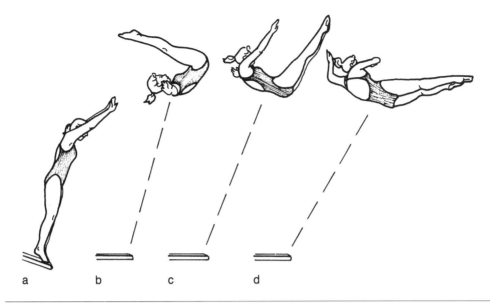

Figure 6.2   Forward somersault with 1 twist—late initiation of twist.

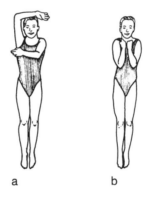

Figure 6.3   Arm positions for twisting: the split arm position (a) and the arms-together position (b).

should reach their lateral positions at the same time. If the diver uses the arms-together technique, the arm on the twisting side must move up the midline of the body to an overhead position, and then out and down laterally to shoulder level. Again, once the top arm starts its move out to the side, the opposite arm begins to move in a direct line to a straight and lateral location at shoulder level. The square-out technique is illustrated in Figure 6.4, a-c. While the arms unwind from the twist position, the body must remain in a straight line with the head neutral, because any movement in these areas will cause a wobbly finish.

Once the diver can successfully perform this skill on the trampoline and the 1-meter springboard, the next step is to learn to twist earlier in the somersault. The diver does this by starting the open-pike somersault, getting a clear look at the lower legs, and then initiating the twist immediately. Because the diver is already accustomed to opening the body as the twist starts, from the "late" twist technique practiced previously, a reflex straightening of the body will occur. The diver should time the twist so it takes place at the 1/2-somersault position. Study Figure 6.5, a-f, to see the sequence of movements.

Figure 6.4 Square-out technique.

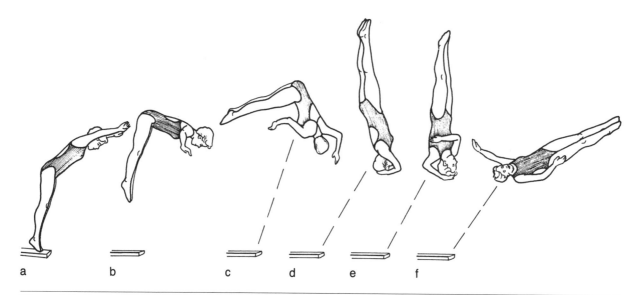

Figure 6.5 Forward somersault with 1 twist—inverted twist.

If the diver can perform this inverted twist technique effectively, he or she can use the dive in competition by bringing the arms down from their lateral location prior to the entry and placing them straight at the sides.

The Forward 1-1/2 Somersault with 1 Twist

This dive is easiest learned from the 3-meter board, because this gives the diver plenty of time to complete all the movements correctly without rushing or forcing the dive, which is often the case when the diver attempts this dive first at the 1-meter level. There is no difference between the twisting technique for this dive and the technique for the forward somersault with 1 twist. However, the diver must learn to square out with the arms and move back to an open-pike somersault position to complete the required rotation before stretching for the entry.

The square-out motions are the same as described for the forward somersault dive. As the arms unwind from the twist and the diver reaches the 7/8-twist point, he or she begins a pike action at the hips. This movement is timed so the diver assumes the finish of the pike as the arms reach their lateral location. The diver must keep the head neutral and resist the temptation to look for the entry before completing the square-out. If the dive is performed correctly, the diver should see the toes and the water directly in front, when he or she assumes the open-pike position. Analyze this dive and especially the square-out sequence carefully in Figure 6.6, a-g. The diver should use the same technique to finish all headfirst twisting dives, regardless of direction of somersault (forward, backward, reverse, or inward). Do not move on to another twisting dive until the diver masters the square-out on this dive.

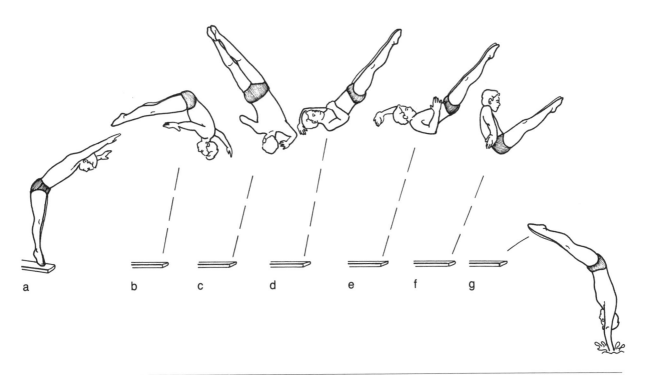

Figure 6.6   Forward 1-1/2 somersault with 1 twist from 1-meter height.

Once the diver performs this dive well at the 3-meter level, he or she can perform the dive from the 1-meter board if capable of completing the dive with good technique.

Performing Multiple Twists

The square-out in the forward somersault twisting dives and the forward 1-1/2-somersault twisting dives should occur no later than completion of the first somersault. If the number of twists is increased, then the diver must initiate the twist earlier and with greater speed in order for the square-out to take place at the correct time. Also, because the diver will be in the straight position longer while executing additional twists, he or she will need more somersault momentum to complete the necessary rotation. This all means that to move from a full twisting somersault or 1-1/2 somersault to a double or triple twist, the diver must do several things as the number of twists increase: create more somersault force from the board, not go as deep into the open-pike position, open the pike to initiate the twist earlier, and develop more twisting force. Because the pike is not as deep or long in the multiple twisting dives, it's not possible for the diver to look at the legs before twisting.

Look at Figure 6.7, a-h, and compare the starting position and the point in the somersault where twist is initiated with the starting position and twist initiation for the forward 1-1/2-somersault dive with 1 twist in Figure 6.6.

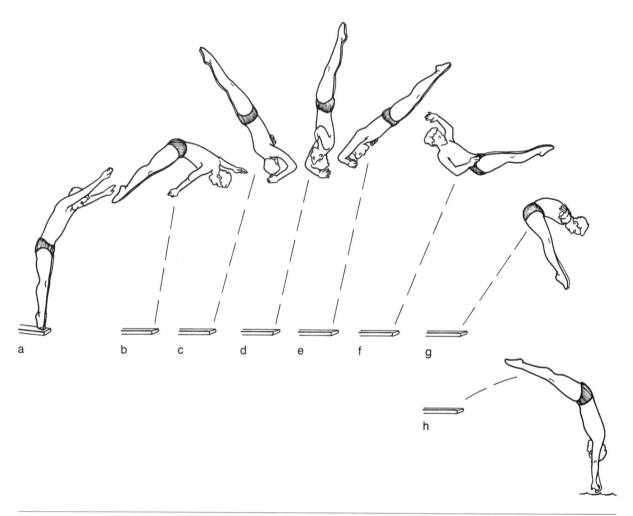

Figure 6.7 Forward 1-1/2 somersault with 2 twists from 1-meter height.

The recommended progression of skills for the forward somersault with 2, 3, or even 4 twists is for the diver to learn these skills first on a trampoline in a spotting belt, and then transfer them to a 1-meter springboard. For the forward 1-1/2-somersault dive with multiple twists, the diver should again learn the basic somersault with twists on a trampoline, then move to the lead-up skill of a somersault with 2, 3, or 4 twists on the 1-meter board. When execution there is good, the diver can take the dive to the 3-meter board. For the forward 1-1/2-somersault dive with 2 or 3 twists, when the diver can do these well from the 3-meter board and has sufficient strength and elevation from the board, he or she can try these dives on the 1-meter board.

Flying Somersault Method

Learning to do a good flying forward somersault is necessary before attempting to twist. The diver can learn the flying somersault on the trampoline with spotting equipment, or on the 1-meter springboard. Figure 6.8, a-f, illustrates this dive.

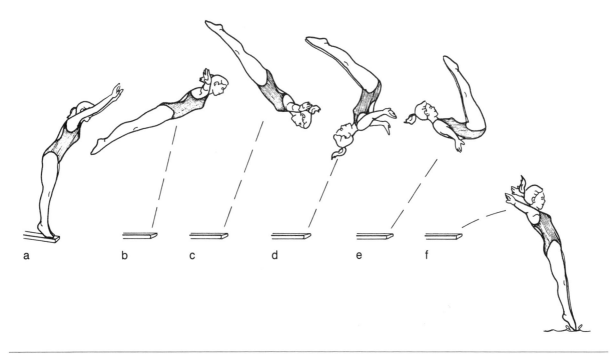

a   b   c   d   e   f

Figure 6.8   Forward flying somersault pike.

The diver leaves the board with the arms overhead and some pike at the hips, which is needed to create the somersault rotation. However, the amount of pike in the one-piece throwing movement should be as little as possible so the diver can keep the upper body, head, and arms at a high angle of takeoff. As the diver leaves the board, the body straightens quickly, the arms move laterally down to shoulder level, and the head remains neutral with the eyes fixed on the far side of the pool. As the dive rotates to an inverted 1/2-somersault position, no movement should occur, but the eyes shift their focus to the entry point. At the 1/2-somersault point, the diver moves to an open-pike position to complete the somersault.

When the diver can perform this skill easily and effectively, the twist can be added. The diver leaves the takeoff point with the head neutral, the eyes looking straight ahead, and the arms overhead. Instead of spreading the arms to a lateral shoulder-high position as in the flying somersault, the diver begins to rotate the arms, head, and upper body in the direction of twist. As in the open-pike twist method, the diver keeps the head neutral and moves the arms initially out and around the body at chest level before bringing them in to the twisting position. As you can see in Figure 6.9, a-g, the square-out and open-pike finish occur much earlier in the somersault with this technique; however the motions of squaring out of the twist are the same.

Increasing the Number of Twists

As with the open-pike twisting method, when the diver wants to add twists to the dive, he or she must create more somersault momentum at the takeoff so as

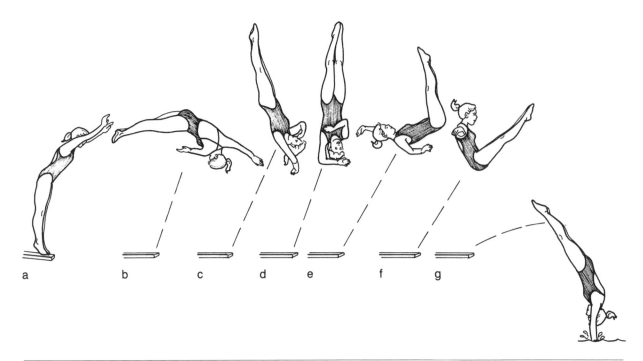

Figure 6.9   Forward 1-1/2 somersault with 1 twist, flying somersault start from 1-meter height.

to be in the straight position longer to complete the twists. Obviously, as the number of twists performed increases, additional twisting force and resultant increased speed of twist are important. However, unlike the open-pike method, the twist does not have to be initiated earlier in the somersault, because it already is early. Adding twists means the diver will square out later in the somersault.

Forward 2-1/2 Somersault With 1 Twist

This dive can be executed in two distinctly different ways. The first method is called the "full twist-in" forward 2-1/2-somersault, which refers to the fact that the diver does the twist at the beginning of the somersaulting action. The second technique is termed the "full twist-out" forward 2-1/2-somersault which means the diver does the twist in the second somersault while coming out of the spin.

Full Twist-In

Essentially this dive is a forward 1-1/2-somersault with 1 twist and another somersault added at the end. The additional somersault can be performed either tuck or pike. Regardless of the position chosen, the diver must finish the twist early in the forward 1-1/2 somersault with 1 twist portion of the dive, and the square-out action must occur with the legs at the horizontal position or even above the horizontal. This makes assuming either the tuck or pike position easier, because the hands and arms can get a better grasp on the legs, resulting in a tighter position.

The critical part of this dive is the movement from the twist to the last somersault. It is here that divers get an off-axis or unsquare direction of rotation to complete the dive. Because there is not enough time to finish the square-out action, as there is in the forward 1-1/2 somersault with 1 twist, the diver must do an abbreviated or 1/2 squaring motion. The diver brings the arm (the one on the side to which the twist is done) over the head and out, moving the arm along the square-out path until it is in line with the shoulder or slightly beyond. The other arm moves laterally so the hand is in line with the shoulder and at chest level, with the elbow bent and close to the body. As this opening occurs the body completes the last 1/2 twist, and the diver quickly grabs the legs to assume the tuck or pike position.

If the diver performs a tuck, the knees must be bent and the legs drawn to the body as the hands move down to grasp the shins; for the pike, the legs are kept straight and lifted.

During this transition from twisting to somersaulting, a diver can make two major mistakes, which will result in a lopsided spin.

1. The lead arm in the square-out movement does not move overhead and out to the shoulder line on the normal square-out path, but moves down and across the front of the body to grab the legs. This movement causes an action–reaction situation. As the arm moves down and across in front of the body, the legs react and shift in the opposite direction, making a square final somersault impossible.
2. The diver draws the legs up toward the body to assume the tuck or pike position, before the hips rotate to the full twist position during the abbreviated squaring action of the arms. This causes the legs to be out of line—in the opposite direction of the twist.

The full twist-in 2-1/2-somersault technique is shown in Figure 6.10, a-j.

If spotting apparatus is available, the diver should learn the forward double somersault with 1 twist on the trampoline first, followed by a forward 2-1/2 somersault with 1 twist. Next have the diver move to the 1-meter board and perform a forward double somersault with 1 twist. When this is done well, the diver can try the forward 2-1/2 somersault with 1 twist on the 3-meter board.

Full Twist-Out

To perform the full twist-out, the diver performs the twist during the second somersault and finishes with a square-out action to an open-pike position, to finish the dive just like the forward 1-1/2 somersault with 1 twist. The diver can start the dive in either tuck or pike position, and there are advantages and disadvantages to both. The tuck spin moves faster, making it easier for the diver to complete the dive; using the tuck makes it more difficult for the diver to initiate the twisting action. Using the pike position makes it harder for the diver to rotate but easier to start the twisting action. I suggest the diver learn this dive first with the tuck; the diver can try the pike later if he or she is strong enough to complete the dive.

Regardless of spinning position, the diver must kick out to a straight body line at approximately the 1-1/2-somersault position and must perform the twist in an inverted position. When initiating the twist, the diver must follow the same principle, presented earlier, of opening the body and twisting simultaneously. As the legs come out of the tuck or pike, the diver will turn the upper body and arms in the twisting direction and then bring them into one of the two arm placement positions described previously. If the kick-out takes place first, the twist will finish late and generally will be slow, because the somersaulting momentum throws the diver into an arched position.

The square-out method to finish this dive is the same as for a forward 1-1/2-somersault dive with 1 twist. The complete sequence of movements for the full twist-out 2-1/2-somersault is shown in Figure 6.11, a-j.

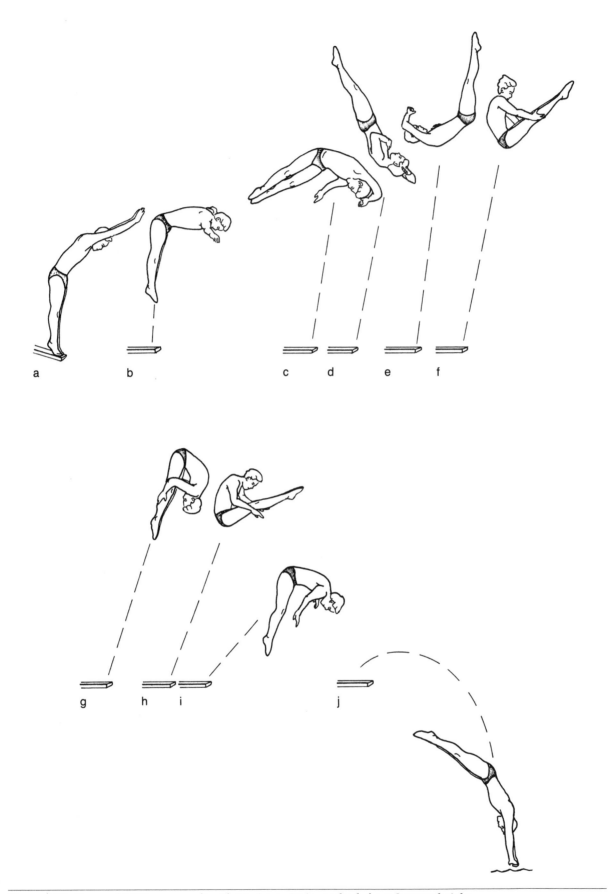

Figure 6.10 Forward 2-1/2 somersault with 1 twist, twist-in method, from 3-meter height.

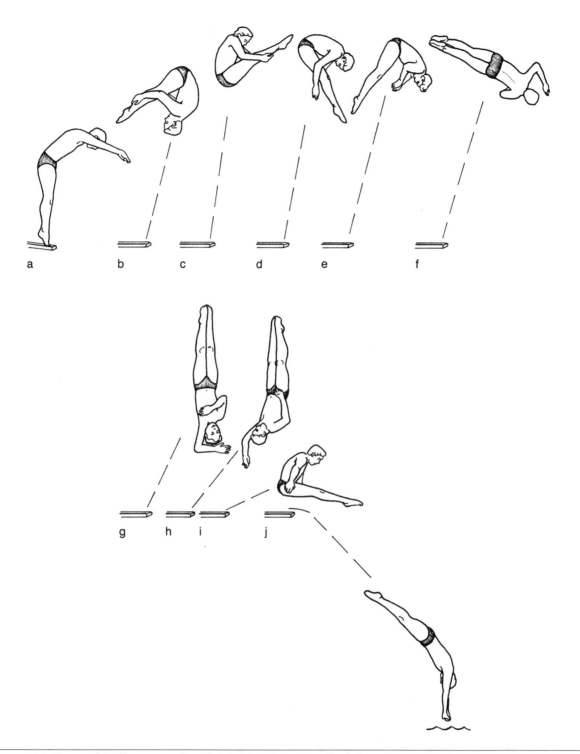

Figure 6.11   Forward 2-1/2 somersault with 1 twist, twist-out method, from 3-meter height.

Forward 2-1/2 Somersault With 2 Twists

Like the forward 2-1/2 somersault with 1 twist, this dive can be done with double twist-in or double twist-out technique. In either case, this is an extremely difficult dive that requires great strength, speed, and lift from the springboard.

Double Twist-In

When broken down into parts, this dive is a forward 1-1/2 somersault with 2 twists followed by another somersault. It is performed the same as the full twist-in forward 2-1/2 somersault, with the exception of the added twist. In order to make the transition from twisting to somersaulting, the diver must complete the double twist at the same point in the somersault as for the 1-twist dive. To accomplish this, the diver must develop more somersault rotation from the springboard and perform an earlier and faster twist. This requirement makes this dive extremely difficult.

Double Twist-Out

The diver executes the double twist-out the same as the full twist-out with regard to moving from the somersault to the twisting action and then squaring out to finish the dive. The addition of the 2nd twist, however, requires that the diver create a stronger somersault rotation at the beginning of the dive to allow time to complete the dive. Also, in order to do 2 twists in time to perform a good square-out finish, the diver must kick out of the spin at approximately the 1-3/8-somersault position. The diver should follow the same progression of lead-up skills when learning these dives as presented for the forward 2-1/2 somersault with 1 twist.

BACKWARD TWISTING DIVES

The twisting techniques are the same for backward and reverse somersaulting dives. Only the takeoff mechanics differ, as described in chapter 5. For this reason, the techniques discussed in this section will apply to both types of dives.

The diver should master the backward twisting dives before attempting the reverse twisters, because for the former dives it is easier to rotate the somersault, and achieving safe distance from the board is not a factor. When the diver can do the backward twisting dives well and complete them easily, he or she can perform the reverse twisting dives, provided the diver has good balance and control of distance on reverse optional dives.

Backward/Reverse Hollow Somersault

For many years diving professionals thought that the backward/reverse somersault in straight position was the basic foundational skill leading to the twisting dives. Recently, a refinement of that skill has been developed that better relates to the actual feeling the diver wants to achieve when doing a twisting dive.

If a diver does a backward/reverse somersault in the straight position, the normal sequence of movements is to swing the arms overhead during the takeoff and arch the body with the head up and pulling in the somersault direction. The diver then maintains this position throughout the dive. However, when the diver does a twisting dive, keeping the body arched and the head pulling backward through the dive is not the desired action; this causes a wobbly slow twist to occur. The diver really needs to start a somersault in the straight position with the arms overhead, the body arched, and the chin up—until leaving the board. At this point, as the twist begins, the body should change to a straight-line shape and the head should move into a neutral position.

That is what happens, but to a greater degree, when the diver does a hollow somersault. This skill starts like the backward/reverse somersault in straight position. As the feet leave the board, the head and upper body stop pulling backward and curl forward into a concave shape as the rest of the body rotates into the somersault. The arms are allowed to relax and drift out to a lateral position during the hollowing action. If performing the dive correctly, the diver will see the legs and feet as they rotate through the 3/8-somersault area and will follow them to the point where he or she can see the water below (see Figure 6.12, a-f).

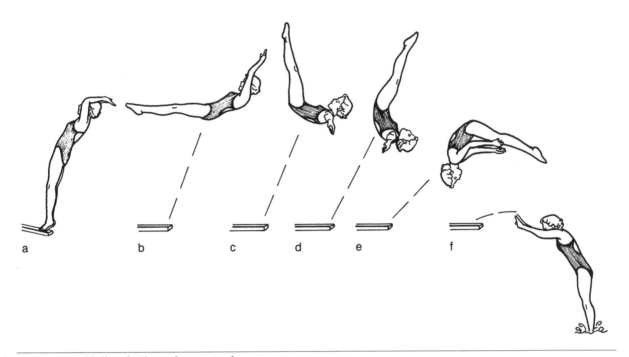

Figure 6.12   Hollow backward somersault.

The diver cannot use this hollow position in its pure form described above, or a wobbly twist will occur because the body is not a straight line. However, the feeling this type of somersault gives the diver—of having the head fixed in one place while the rest of the body rotates around it—can be transferred to the twisting dives if the diver thinks of hollowing the body shape and keeping the head position neutral at the correct time. This will be discussed as each dive is explained.

Before beginning the discussion of the complex multiple backward twisting dives, we need to address a more basic type of twisting dive that can be used at all diving levels.

Backward/Reverse Somersault or 1-1/2- Somersault With 1/2 Twist

These dives can be performed with one of two methods: the single-arm turn or the double-arm turn. Regardless of which technique is chosen, the diver must learn the hollow backward/reverse somersault first to establish the correct head and body position when starting the twist.

Single-Arm Turn

To perform the backward/reverse 1- or 1-1/2-somersault with 1/2 twist using the single-arm turn action, the diver executes the following sequence of movements. The diver establishes the takeoff position as the feet are ready to leave the board, with the body arched, the arms extended straight and parallel overhead, and the head between the arms with the chin up and the eyes looking up. Just after the feet leave the board, the head and upper body become fixed in their position and the beginning of the hollow somersault feeling occurs. Simultaneously the diver bends the arm on the twisting side and brings it down in front of the body to a position in front of the chest with the elbow flexed approximately 90 degrees. The other arm remains stretched overhead. This movement causes the twist to begin in the direction of the dropped arm. Due to the movement toward a hollow somersault position as the diver starts the twist, the body should move from an arched to a straight shape and the head should be in a neutral position. These two factors contribute to a twisting action that is smooth and flat, rather than arched and wobbly.

When the twist nears the 1/2-twist point, the diver straightens the arm located across the chest and moves it horizontally to a lateral shoulder-high position; at the same time the arm overhead moves down in line with the body, to the same place on the opposite side. At the end of the arm movement to the lateral position, the diver can move the body to a tuck or pike position by drawing the legs into the body. The diver can then finish the dive by grabbing the shins in a tuck or grabbing the back of the legs in a closed pike, or can simply remain with the arms to the side in an open-pike position (which is the easiest and most popular method). Depending on the dive being performed, the diver can then either open to a feetfirst entry or rotate to the headfirst position.

Figure 6.13, a-e, shows the single-arm turn technique. Regardless of direction of rotation or number of somersaults done, the key requirements for good execution are the same: The diver should

- establish a square line of somersault from the board with both arms overhead at takeoff;
- perform a slight hollow motion as the arm on the twisting side moves down in front of the chest; and
- execute the tuck or pike finish at the end of the arm action. Moving from the straight body shape to the tuck or pike too early will cause an off-axis dive on entry.

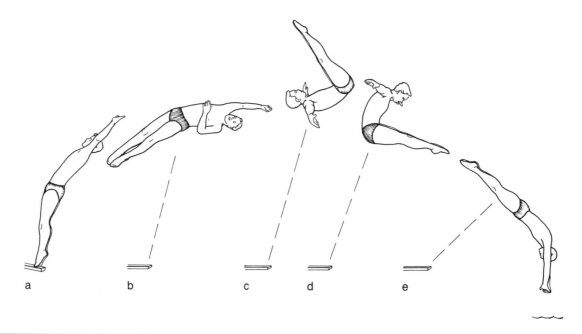

Figure 6.13 Backward 1-1/2 somersault with 1/2 twist, single-arm turn technique from 1-meter height.

Double-Arm Turn

The takeoff position for this technique is the same as for the single-arm turn. As the feet leave the board, the diver keeps the arms straight and parallel overhead as the shoulders and upper body turn in the direction of the twist and the body moves from an arched position to a straight line with the head in a neutral position. The movement of the upper body combined with the already established somersault momentum causes the body to twist. The diver holds this position until a 1/2 twist is completed. The diver now can finish the dive by moving directly to a tuck, pike, or open-pike position for the remainder of the somersault, or the diver can spread the arms to a lateral position and perform a flying somersault action before assuming a body position for the completion of the dive.

If the diver chooses to move directly to the somersault position, he or she should move the arms and legs in a direct line to the desired tuck or closed pike, or should spread the arms laterally while moving the legs to the open-pike position.

When performing the flying somersault action in the middle of the transition from twist to somersault, the diver must hold the body straight as the arms move to their lateral position. The diver fixes the line of sight momentarily on the entry point below, until the movement to the tuck, pike, or open pike is made. Figure 6.14, a-g, shows the double-arm turn technique.

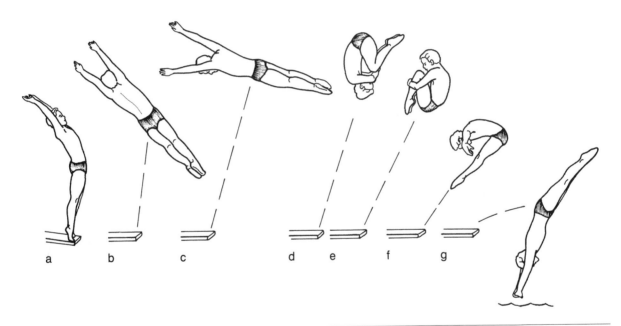

Figure 6.14 Reverse 1-1/2 somersault with 1/2 twist in tuck position, double-arm turn technique from 1-meter height.

Any of these techniques are acceptable and can equally help the diver score well when executed properly. Which method is used depends on the level of the springboard or platform the diver uses, how much time the diver has for making the movements, and which technique the diver can do best. Obviously, the flying somersault action takes the most time to perform, and the diver must take this into account when making a choice.

Backward Somersault With 1-1/2 Twists

The sequence of movements used to execute this dive is the same for all the multiple twisting dives. Once the diver correctly learns the skills for the 1-1/2-

twist dive, the door is opened to effectively adding more twists later, if the diver has sufficient strength, quickness, and elevation from the board.

As with forward twisting, the best way for the diver to learn the movements for a 1-1/2 twist is by using the trampoline with overhead spotting equipment. Once the diver masters skills in this situation, transferring the dive to the 1-meter board is an easy task. If a trampoline and spotting equipment are not available, then the diver must perform the same learning sequence on the board.

The hollow somersault is the foundation for the start of this dive. Whether doing backward or reverse twisting dives, the diver must perform the corresponding hollow somersault correctly and complete it relatively easily before attempting twisting actions. If the diver is struggling to execute the basic somersault, delay working on the twist, because the diver will compensate correct technique just to be able to complete the dive.

There are 4 steps in the teaching process for the backward somersault with 1-1/2 twists.

Step 1   The diver does a hollow back somersault (review Figure 6.12). This is the lead-up skill before the diver attempts twisting. It reinforces the feeling the diver should have of keeping the head and upper body stationary as the rest of the body rotates. This skill also helps the diver determine the speed of the somersault for Step 2.

Step 2   The diver starts a hollow somersault. After the arms reach the overhead takeoff position and the feet leave the trampoline or springboard, the diver begins the twisting movement by dropping the arm on the twisting side (left arm if twisting left, and vice versa). The diver drops this arm down and back with the elbow bent, so it points to the trampoline bed or the water, directly behind and a few feet from the takeoff point. The head and upper body follow the arm with a turning motion in the same direction, while the other arm remains extended overhead. As the twist begins, the diver should use the action of the hollow somersault to change from an arched to a straight body line.

After several attempts, the diver should be able to complete a somersault with 1/2 twist. Work on this phase of starting the twist should continue until refinement of the movements allows the diver to accomplish 3/4 to 1 twist without making any added movements of the arms. The arms should remain with one arm up and one arm down, and both away from the body, throughout the twist.

You can assist the diver with verbal commands, which help him or her concentrate on the right move at the right time. Just prior to extension for the takeoff into the somersault, give the command "hollow"; just as the takeoff occurs, use the cue "drop." If you give these commands right before the action being targeted is to occur, the diver can be jolted into concentration on that skill and still have adequate time to react at the correct moment. Figure 6.15, a-g, shows the backward somersault with 1 twist.

Step 3   The diver performs the same movements as in Step 2 and, at approximately the 1/2 twist position, moves the arms into the twisting position. The diver should bring the top (overhead) arm down and across the chest so the hand rests just below the opposite armpit; he or she should also move the bottom arm directly upward and over the head so the upper arm is against the side of the head and the forearm rests on top of the head. The diver must

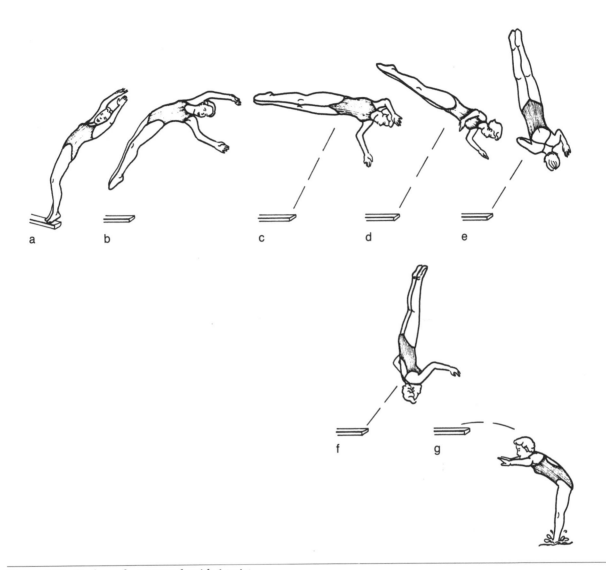

Figure 6.15 Backward somersault with 1 twist.

move the bottom arm in an upward and backward direction, to guard against that arm coming in front of the face to reach its destination. The head should remain still throughout this arm movement, and the body should remain straight.

Again, verbal commands can be helpful. Give the same "hollow" and "drop" cues as in Step 2, and add a third command—"wrap"—to signal the time to move the arms into the twist position.

The diver needs to practice this step until he or she can perform 1-1/2 twists (see Figure 6.16, a-g).

Step 4   Now that the diver can do 1-1/2 twists, he or she must stop the twists using the same square-out action as described for the forward twisting dives. The arm over the head moves in an upward and lateral path out and down to shoulder level, with the arm straight. The arm across the chest moves in a direct line to a straight position at shoulder level. The head should remain in a neutral position throughout the squaring action.

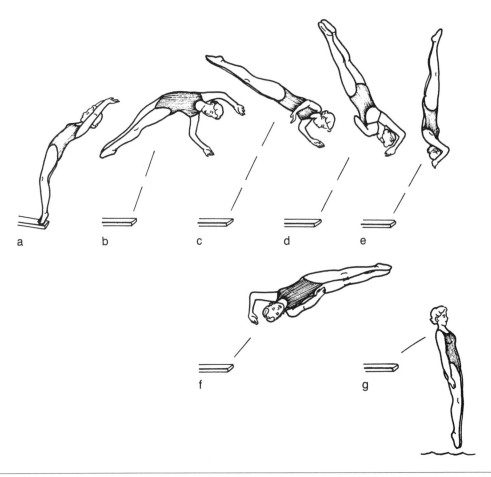

Figure 6.16   Backward somersault with 1-1/2 twists.

If the diver chooses the other arm-twisting position (arms together), Steps 1 and 2 are performed the same; the difference occurs in Step 3, when the arms are "wrapped" into the body. For the beginner, the split arm–twisting position is best for accelerating the twist and easier for squaring out. Regardless of which arm position the diver utilizes, keep in mind the concept presented earlier in the chapter: Moving the arms out and around the upper body and then to the twisting position is the effective way for the diver to twist, rather than pulling the arms directly into the body.

Refining the Backward Twisting Movement

It is now time to insert one additional movement that makes the twisting action more efficient. The reason you should not introduce this factor in the initial learning stage is that it will confuse the beginner and interfere with progress at that stage. However, once the diver learns the basic twisting movements effectively, this step can be added with little problem.

Refer to Step 2 of the step-by-step teaching progression, when the diver drops the arm on the twisting side down and back to point at the trampoline or water behind the takeoff. At this point the head is turned in the direction of twist as the arm drops. The diver should touch the chin to the shoulder and focus the line of sight down that arm to the trampoline or water beyond. The eyes continue to focus on that point as the arms begin their movement into the twisting position.

This slight hesitation and visual focusing allow the body to catch up to the head position and also allow the head to move to a neutral position for the remainder of the twist.

This turning of the head provides added momentum to the twisting action, and when the diver visually spots the water behind (the springboard for reverse twisting dives), this head movement aids in the hollowing action of the body, causing an earlier acceleration of the twist. The diver should sight the same reference point on each takeoff for consistency of movement. Also, the diver must not throw the head back, looking over the top of the shoulder or overhead, but rather should turn in a direct line to the shoulder.

As an added action to assist the acceleration of the twist, the diver can bend the elbow of the lead arm approximately 45 degrees as it points to the trampoline or water; this accelerates the wrapping in of the arms to the body. Figure 6.17, a and b, shows the lead arm action during backward twisting.

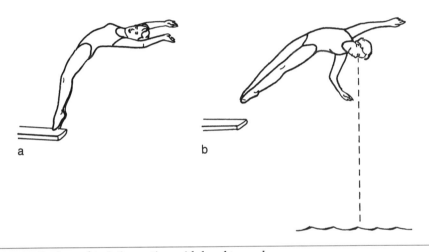

Figure 6.17 Backward twisting action with head turned.

Remember, first teach the basic movements outlined in Steps 1 through 4, then add these refinements as the diver's proficiency warrants. If confusion results, stay with the fundamental movements until the diver is ready to try the refinements.

Backward 1-1/2 Somersault With 1-1/2 Twists

Once the diver can perform the backward somersault with 1-1/2 twists from the 1-meter springboard, he or she can then use this dive in competition by moving the arms down to the sides after the square-out and entering the water feetfirst.

For the next progression, the diver learns the backward 1-1/2 somersault with 1-1/2 twists. This is best done from the 3-meter board first, so the diver has adequate time to execute all the movements without rushing. When the diver can perform the dive effectively from the 3-meter level, it can then be done from the 1-meter board, if the diver is physically capable.

Moving from the somersault to the 1-1/2 somersault requires the same technique as described for the forward 1-1/2 somersault with 1 twist; you may want to review this technique. The entire backward 1-1/2-somersault with 1-1/2 twists is shown in Figure 6.18, a-g.

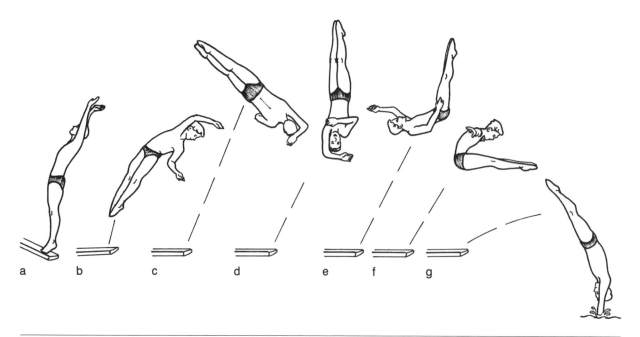

Figure 6.18   Backward 1-1/2 somersault with 1-1/2 twists from 1-meter height.

Reverse Somersault or 1-1/2 Somersault With 1-1/2 Twists

If the diver can correctly demonstrate the backward 1-1/2 somersault with 1-1/2 twists from the 3-meter level, and can perform a good hollow reverse somersault from the 1-meter board, it is time to do the reverse somersault with 1-1/2 twists. Because the diver already knows the twisting technique, he or she can execute this dive by performing the hollow somersault first, as a lead-up skill and to set the speed of somersault rotation, then executing the reverse somersault with 1-1/2 twists from the 1-meter board. When the diver performs this skill well, he or she can perform the reverse 1-1/2 somersault with 1-1/2 twists at the 3-meter height. The entire reverse 1-1/2 somersault with 1-1/2 twists is shown in Figure 6.19, a-h.

Performing Additional Twists

As with the forward twisting dives, the square-out action is extremely difficult for the diver to perform with backward and reverse twisting dives if the somersault rotation passes the 1-somersault position before the diver completes the required number of twists. Actually it is best if the diver can finish the twisting earlier than the first somersault position, for squaring out becomes easier. Usually, this timing is not a problem for dives with 1-1/2 twists. However, when the diver executes 2-1/2 or 3-1/2 twists, timing twists and somersaults is a key factor in successful performance.

When performing additional twists, the diver must do several things in order to complete the required number of rotations before passing the square-out point in the somersault:

1. The diver must create more somersault rotation at takeoff, because he or she will be in the straight body position longer in order to complete the greater number of twists.
2. The diver must twist as early as possible without affecting the axis of somersault rotation; twisting too early causes the diver to somersault from the board sideways. Always emphasize that the diver get the arms to a complete overhead takeoff position before dropping the arm on the twisting side to start the twist.

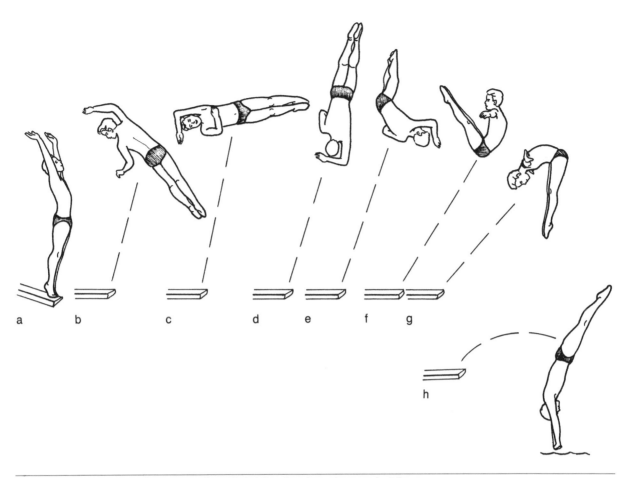

Figure 6.19 Reverse 1-1/2 somersault with 1-1/2 twists from 1-meter height.

3. The diver must develop a faster twist by performing a more forceful turning motion of the arms, head, and upper body into the twist; bending the elbow of the arm leading into the twist more quickly to accelerate the twist earlier; and keeping the arms in, as tight to the body as possible, during the twist.

Because twisting dives involve so many factors that can negatively affect performance, this checklist of common mistakes may help you locate problems.

COMMON PROBLEMS AND CAUSES IN TWISTING DIVES

Problem	Possible Cause
The twist is too slow.	1. The diver does not establish adequate somersault rotation first. 2. The diver brings the arms directly into the body rather than moving them out and around chest first. 3. The diver uses excessive body arch or pike in the twist.

(Cont.)

COMMON PROBLEMS AND
CAUSES IN TWISTING DIVES (Continued)

Problem	Possible Cause
	4. The diver holds the elbows significantly away from the body in the twist.
	5. The diver inadequately turns the arms, head, and upper body to initiate twist.
The twist is wobbly.	1. The body position is arched, piked, or tilted laterally in the upper body.
	2. Head position is forward, backward, or tilted laterally toward a shoulder.
	3. The elbows stick out too far.
The finish is not square.	1. The somersault is off axis or the diver jumps to one side or the other on takeoff.
	2. The diver drops the head down and forward in the square-out, thus seeing the water below, before finishing the square-out motion.
	3. The diver moves the top or lead arm in the square-out, down and forward in front of the body.
	4. The diver moves the arm across the chest toward the entry before finishing the square-out, or sets the arm behind the body rather than in a lateral placement.
	5. The diver pikes at the hips in the square-out before completing the last 1/8 of the twist.
	6. The diver finishes the twist beyond the 1-somersault point of rotation.
	7. The diver squares out too late; he or she should begin this action in the last 1/4 portion of the desired number of twists.

CALLING TWISTERS

Most divers like the security of verbal cues during their first attempts at new dives. Because the squaring out action for twisting dives begins during the last 3/8 to 1/4 twist of the dive, you should give the verbal call to come out of the twist just as the diver enters the last 1/2 twist of the dive. This gives the diver time to react to the command and begin the square-out at the appropriate point. Usually after only a couple of calls, the diver will perform the dive successfully with no assistance.

SUMMARY

Patience in teaching and learning the twisting dives is extremely important to successful execution of the complicated maneuvers required. The diver must learn each prerequisite skill correctly before moving to the next step. Basic flaws in execution or twist position may become permanent if not corrected early. Diligence in the beginning stages of learning will be rewarded with beautiful, flowing, spectacular twisting dives.

7
CHAPTER

PLATFORM DIVING

Platform diving is easier and less complicated than springboard diving because the takeoff surface is stationary. This eliminates many of the balance and timing problems that are so frustrating in springboard diving. However, the platform diver needs the courage to perform dives at the higher heights, and the physical strength and durability to absorb the impact with the water, especially from the 7-1/2- and 10-meter platforms.

If the diver develops good springboard skills first, learning platform diving is much simpler. The balance and control needed for the takeoff, correct mechanics of execution, spatial orientation in the dives, and entry techniques of springboard diving all transfer to platform diving. A good springboard background is a valuable foundation for the platform event.

Because the techniques of executing the dives are the same for springboard and platform diving, it is not necessary to discuss the mechanics of the dives in this chapter (with the exception of the armstand group). The focus here will be on discussing the skills every diver should learn at the 1-meter, 3-meter, and 5-meter levels before moving up to 7-1/2- and 10-meter heights.

SPRINGBOARD VERSUS PLATFORM

There are some definite differences in performing the same dive on the springboard versus the platform. Because the platform does not assist the diver's rotation, dives on the platform feel "dead"; they don't have the same zip or feeling of speed in the spin as springboard dives. For this reason, beginning divers often think they are "stuck" in the spin, that is, not rotating fast enough. With experience the diver will adjust to this different feeling. The general rule is that if the dive feels too slow by springboard standards, it's probably just right.

Due to the heights of the takeoff from the water at the 5-, 7-1/2- and 10-meter levels, the time of drop to the water after the diver completes the dive is longer than on the springboard. This is especially true for the basic dives and easier optionals, so the diver must adjust the point at which the stretch for the entry begins.

Finally, the takeoff occurs more quickly from the platform. Because the surface does not move, the diver must crouch down and jump with great speed to develop elevation and rotation. The period of time when the springboard is depressed and then recoils is eliminated. When moving from springboard to platform diving, divers describe the difference in takeoff as switching from the slow mode to the fast mode.

CONTROL OF TAKEOFFS

When divers move to higher and higher platform levels, they normally become somewhat afraid and therefore tentative in initiating their dives. This usually results in increased lean from the platform and a delayed push-off with the legs, both of which actions cause a loss of control. The greater the lean, the greater the somersault rotation. When the diver leans away first and then pushes with the legs and moves the upper body into the rotational motion, the spin is whiplike and uncontrolled.

To avoid this situation, teach the beginner to jump strongly and boldly from the platform no matter what its height. A strong jump in the takeoff is the key to controlled dives whether the diver is performing a basic dive or an optional. If you preach this concept from the start of the platform diver's training, it will become ingrained and will not be a problem. This is a good reason to start the diver from deck level—or from a low-level (1/2-, 1-, or 3-meter) platform—with the basic takeoffs, jumps, and dives, before moving to the 5-meter height and beyond.

Keep in mind also that among the criteria evaluated by judges are strength and aggressiveness of the takeoff. This is a very important reason for emphasizing a bold attitude in the beginning platform diver.

THE TAKEOFFS

Seven basic takeoffs can be done from the platform: standing forward, running forward, backward, standing reverse, running reverse, inward, and armstand. We will discuss these in the order in which they should be learned. All the takeoffs, with the exception of the running reverse, should be practiced from the 1-, 3-, and 5-meter heights. The diver should practice the running reverse takeoff at the 1-meter level until he or she is more advanced and ready to combine this takeoff with a dive. If a 1-meter platform is not available, the diver can practice takeoffs from the pool deck if it has a safe, nonskid surface.

Standing Reverse Takeoff

This takeoff is done with a jump and is really a forward-type takeoff that becomes a reverse takeoff when combined with a reverse rotating dive at a later time.

The diver stands at the end of the platform facing forward, with the head erect, eyes sighting downward to the water, body aligned, arms at the sides, and feet together with the toes even with the edge of the platform. Many divers curl their toes over the edge to get a good grip; however, this technique contributes to jumping too far away from the platform on takeoff, because the diver can lean forward and push off the forward edge. When the toes are even with the edge, the diver must push up off the top of the platform surface.

The diver performs the press with the same motions as the 2-part press described for backward takeoffs in springboard diving. The arms lift laterally and slightly in front of the body to a position approximately 45 degrees above horizontal. As the arms pass shoulder height, the ankles extend, the diver rises up on the toes, and the body stretches upward, while the center of balance shifts forward over the front of the feet so good distance will be achieved. Then the arms begin to circle back and down as the body crouches into a jumping position, and the heels come back down on the platform. As the arms pass the legs and begin the swing up, the body extends. At the point of takeoff, the body is in a straight line angled slightly forward and the arms are straight and parallel in an overhead position (see Figure 7.1, a-h).

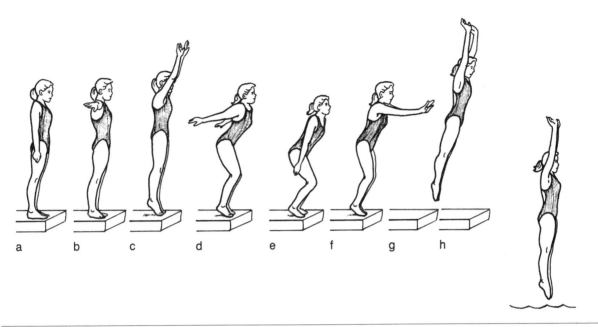

Figure 7.1 Standing reverse takeoff with jump.

At a more advanced stage when the diver is preparing to do a reverse dive, he or she can do a reverse jump from the pool deck or 1-meter level as a lead-up skill. Just before the feet leave the platform, the diver drives the hips forward and upward causing the body to arch and causing some reverse rotation, so the diver can enter the water feetfirst at a 45-degree angle backward toward the platform (see Figure 7.2, a-h).

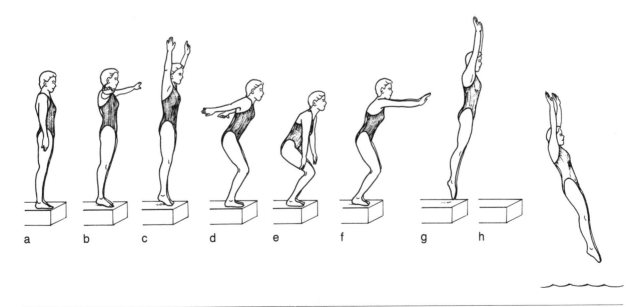

Figure 7.2 Standing reverse takeoff with reverse jump.

Backward Takeoff

This takeoff utilizes the same movements as the reverse takeoff. The diver stands backward on the edge of the platform with one third to one half of each foot on the platform and the heels slightly above platform level. The diver then executes the 2-part press with two key points in mind. First, as the body moves down into the crouched jumping position, the weight shifts backward through the hips, and the shoulders and upper body stay over the platform. This gives the diver proper distance in the takeoff. Second, the heels remain slightly higher than the level of the platform at the bottom of the press, so the diver can maintain balance correctly. If the heels drop below platform height, the diver will fall backward too far.

As the arms swing up, the body extends and the diver leaves the platform into a backward jump with the body straight and the arms straight and parallel overhead (see Figure 7.3, a-h). When the diver passes the platform, if correct distance has been achieved, the diver should be able to reach out and touch the edge of the platform with the fingertips. This is a good way to check the distance.

a   b   c   d   e   f   g   h

Figure 7.3   Backward takeoff with jump.

Standing Forward Takeoff

The diver stands on the front edge of the platform just as for the reverse takeoff, then lifts the arms laterally to a straight and parallel position directly overhead. To start the takeoff movement, the diver rises high on the toes, stretches the arms and body upward, and shifts the body weight forward over the toes farther than in the standing reverse takeoff, to ensure safe distance. The head stays level and the eyes focus downward to the water. Then the diver bends the body at the hips and knees to prepare for the takeoff, while the arms remain still and the heels drop down for a strong springing action; however, the heels do not touch the platform. The diver then extends the body into a jump with the arms held overhead (see Figure 7.4, a-f).

Figure 7.4   Standing forward takeoff with jump.

Inward Takeoff

There are two methods of performing the inward takeoff. The diver should learn these while doing a backward jump and then should also use them at a later stage with an inward dive, which will be described in another section. The technique that the diver should learn first starts with the arms held straight overhead. The body is straight, the heels are level or slightly above the platform, and one third to one half of the feet are placed on the platform. The head stays level with the eyes sighting halfway down the runway. To start the takeoff, the diver lifts up high on the toes while stretching up through the body, shoulders, and arms to lift his or her center of gravity as high as possible and to put the body in a stretched state. From this high stretched position, the legs and hips bend as the body weight drops downward strongly. The heels move down but stop at a position level with, or slightly above, the platform. The arms should be kept straight, although some divers do cock the arms by bending at the elbows. This is acceptable if the bend is not extreme and the hands remain over the head instead of back behind the body. When the diver reaches the bottom of the sitting position, the legs begin to extend, propelling the diver upward. At the same time, the head, arms, and upper body remain still while the legs drive the hips outward from the platform. These actions allow the diver to perform a jump and to move away from the platform to a safe distance.

The movement of the body in this press is an up-down-up action, which the diver does very quickly to achieve a good bouncing motion and corresponding strong jump from the platform. The amount of knee and hip bend in the downward portion of the takeoff depends on the diver's leg strength and quickness; however, a moderate amount of downward sitting movement is necessary. If the diver goes too deep into the crouching action, he or she will lose the speed of movement, and if the amount of leg bend is too little, a weak jump will result. Experimentation will show the diver how much leg flexion results in the best takeoff.

During the upward and downward phases of the press prior to the jump, the diver must maintain the balance steady over the balls of the feet with no movement either forward or backward. When the diver pushes off in the takeoff, he or she will then move away from the platform by driving backward off the toes with the legs and hips (see Figure 7.5, a-e).

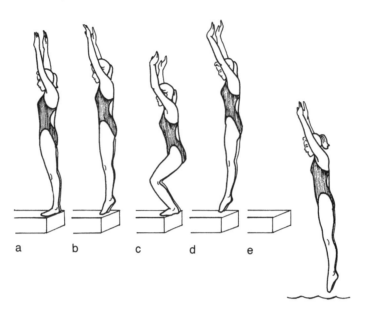

Figure 7.5 Inward takeoff with jump, arms overhead.

When the diver masters the overhead takeoff, he or she can try a slightly different starting position. The diver stands the same way on the platform, except the arms are kept at the sides. Keeping the arms straight, the diver lifts the arms slowly in a lateral path to the overhead position. As the arms pass head level, they move quickly to the straight and parallel overhead position, as the ankles also lift the diver quickly to a position up on the toes. From this point, the takeoff is the same as described before. The advantage of this technique is that it gives the diver a preliminary upward movement of the arms to get the takeoff started; also, the strong, quick upward movement of the arms as they pass head level provides more momentum to help the diver lift the center of gravity as high as possible prior to dropping down into the press. The inward takeoff with jump, with arms starting at the diver's sides, is shown in Figure 7.6, a-g. Either takeoff method is effective, so you and the diver need to try both techniques and select the one that works and feels best.

The diver should practice the forward, backward, reverse, and inward takeoffs with jumps, at all platform levels up to 5 meters, until he or she learns control, balance, and proper distance. Actually, the forward (standing reverse takeoff) and backward jump can also be done at the 7-1/2- and 10-meter heights as preparatory skills for dives to be done later. These jumps acclimate the diver to the higher levels and the timing of the drop to the water, and the jumps also teach balance and the strong jump action needed for control in the other dives. The diver can perform many repetitions of these skills, because there is no problem with the force of the impact with the water causing fatigue as is the case in headfirst entries from these heights.

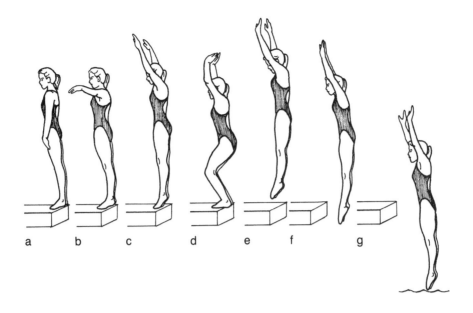

Figure 7.6 Inward takeoff with jump, arms at sides.

Running Forward Takeoff

The forward running approach is a short, dancelike skill that must be shaped to suit the diver's taste and ability. The diver can take 3 or more steps in the approach plus a hurdle to the end of the platform, and the diver can take the steps while either walking or running. There are many variations of the arm swing that can be used, as well as various rhythms and timings. Regardless of what type of approach is developed, the diver should follow certain basic fundamentals in order to accomplish a good takeoff with balance, control, and good distance.

Number of Steps

By rule, the diver must take at least 3 steps and a hurdle. The number of steps should correspond to the springboard approach, so there is no confusion regarding which foot to begin with and which foot to hurdle from. Making the approach in both events similar simplifies the learning process.

Head and Eyes

The diver should keep the head level throughout the approach and the eyes focused on the end of the platform where the landing and takeoff will occur. During the hurdle, just before landing and after the diver has ensured he or she will land on the edge, the vision shifts to the water, while the head stays level and the eyes look down.

Arms

No matter what swing pattern or timing the diver uses, three factors are most important as the diver readies the arms for the takeoff.

1. The arms must reach a position directly over the head in a straight and parallel alignment *before* the feet land for the takeoff. This is necessary

because the takeoff occurs so quickly that effective use of the arms is not possible unless they are in position first.

2. The path of the arms to their overhead position must be lateral. If the arms are brought up in a lateral-forward path, the diver will bend over too much on the takeoff. If the diver brings the arms directly up the front, or if the arms move up laterally behind the body line, a backward lean on takeoff can occur.

3. The arms must be kept straight throughout the approach and takeoff.

Upper Body

The diver should maintain the torso in position slightly forward of vertical throughout the approach and the landing on the end of the platform. As the landing and takeoff take place, the center of balance shifts forward depending on the dive being performed.

Legs

As the hurdle to the end takes place, the legs flex at the hip and knee joints in preparation for the landing. The diver positions the legs in front of the upper body, so they can act as brakes to control the strong horizontal momentum that is present as a result of the run. If the legs were directly under the upper body, the diver either would have to approach the end of the platform very slowly or would lose control too far forward on the takeoff.

Upon landing, the diver should use a minimum amount of additional flexion of the knee and hip joints. A very quick landing of the body weight onto the legs and corresponding recoil into the takeoff should occur. The less time the diver is in contact with the platform, the stronger the jump into the takeoff will be.

Feet

The diver should take the last step prior to the hurdle so the heel contacts the platform first, and then the foot rocks forward until the diver pushes off with the toes to the end of the platform. The diver lands on the end of the platform on the balls of the feet, with the heels slightly elevated so the ankles are prepared for an immediate and explosive extension into the takeoff.

The Hurdle

Unlike springboard diving, platform hurdling is done in a long, low trajectory. As the diver moves through the air after the push-off into the hurdle, the feet should be only a few inches above the platform surface. The length of the hurdle depends on the speed of the approach. Hurdles taken with the walking approach, are 3 to 4 feet long, whereas hurdles taken with the running technique are from 4 to 6 feet in length, with the majority of those in the 4- to 5-foot range.

Keeping all these fundamentals in mind, let's construct the forward platform approach. Whatever approach is selected, the diver should practice it diligently with a forward jump first at the 1-, 3-, and 5-meter levels, and later from the 7-1/2- and 10-meter platforms. The running forward approach with a jump is valuable in teaching the diver balance and control of distance with the increased horizontal velocity, before the diver does any dives.

Walking Method

This is the simplest and easiest approach for the beginner to learn; teach this first before moving to the more difficult running method.

To eliminate confusion, the number of steps the diver takes prior to the hurdle should be the same number he or she uses in the springboard approach. Once the diver determines this number, he or she should mark off the approach on the deck by taking the appropriate number of steps and a low 3- to 4-foot hurdle, taking off from one foot and landing on two feet. During practice, the diver can adjust the length and speed of the approach so it feels good.

The diver must remember one point when marking off any approach: After the diver takes the hurdle and lands, the place where the tip of the big toe lands is where the heels should be placed when the diver turns around to perform the approach in the direction from which it was measured. Failing to do this is a common mistake among divers. They often measure off the approach from the front end of the platform or on the ground, and when they turn around to do the approach in the other direction, they start with their toes at the point where their toes ended up in the mark-off. This mistake adds one full foot length to the approach and makes it more difficult for the divers to be precise in landing on the end of the platform.

To combine the arm and leg actions, the diver should perform the walking approach by lifting the arms straight and laterally, in a gradual movement, during the last 3 steps prior to the hurdle, so the arms are directly overhead when the diver pushes off into the hurdle. If the diver chooses to take only 3 steps, then the arms must begin their lateral and upward movement on the 1st step. When the diver uses the 4-step approach, the arms begin to move in the 2nd step, and for the 5-step approach, they move in the 3rd step. Study the 4-step walking forward approach in Figure 7.7, a-i.

a	b	c	d	e	f	g	h	i

Figure 7.7 Forward approach, walking.

Running Method

There are two basic ways to use the arms in the running approach. The first method is a combination of the forward and backward arm swing and lateral arm lift, whereas the second method involves just forward and backward swings. In both cases, during the final 2 steps prior to the hurdle, the diver brings the arms up laterally to the overhead position just prior to landing on the end of the platform. Therefore, even though the various approaches may appear different, the same fundamentals apply in all cases.

Because divers usually take 3, 4, or 5 steps in the approach, the next sections describe each type of approach as well as both types of arm swing. By using imagination and ingenuity, the diver can take the basic patterns described and create his or her own running takeoff.

3-Step Run.   The diver assumes the stance with the body aligned, the head level, and the eyes focused on the end of the platform. The diver lifts the arms laterally halfway to shoulder height, and while taking the 1st step swings the arms down to the sides and upward and forward to a horizontal and parallel position in front of the body. The diver takes the next 2 steps in a slow running fashion; during Step 2 the arms swing from their forward position back to the sides, and during Step 3 the arms swing in a continuous motion laterally up to shoulder height. The hurdle then begins as the arms continue to move to their straight and parallel alignment overhead; the arms reach this position just before the diver lands back on the platform. The diver should take the 1st step at a moderate speed, and then should change to a loping type of running speed for the next 2 steps (see Figure 7.8, a-i).

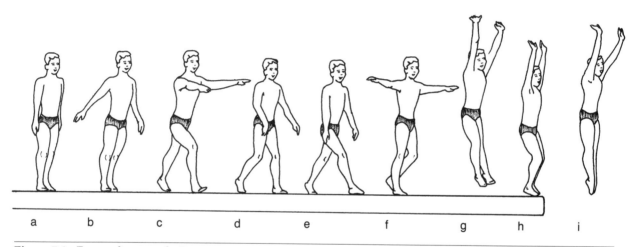

a   b   c   d   e   f   g   h   i

Figure 7.8   Forward approach, 3-step run.

4-Step Run.   Before taking the 1st step, the diver swings the arms forward to a parallel position 45 degrees below horizontal in preparation for the arm movement in the 1st step. As when using the 3-step run, the diver takes the 1st step at a moderate speed. As the step is taken, the arms swing back toward the body and up laterally to shoulder height. In the 2nd step the diver increases speed to a slow running tempo for the remainder of the steps. As the 2nd step occurs, the arms swing down to the sides and in a continuous motion up to a parallel alignment in front of the body at shoulder height. In the 3rd and 4th steps, the arms swing down to the sides and laterally up to shoulder height again. As the hurdle begins, the arms continue to move upward to the overhead position prior to takeoff. The arm patterns allow the approach to be done in a very rhythmic, aesthetic manner, which adds to the grace of the dive (see Figure 7.9, a-k).

If the diver chooses to use this type of arm swing with a 5-step run, he or she should take the first 2 steps at walking speed while the arms move forward in front of the body on Step 1 and back to the sides and laterally up to shoulder height in Step 2. The rest of the run and movements are the same.

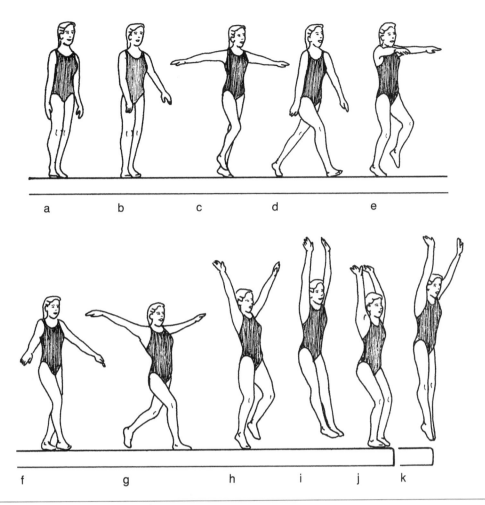

Figure 7.9 Forward approach, 4-step run.

5-Step Run. The following text describes a forward and back arm-swing action for a 5-step approach. Although there is some difference in the first 3 steps, the arm action in the last 2 steps and the hurdle are the same as for the 3- and 4-step approaches.

The diver takes the 1st step at walking speed, keeping the arms parallel and swung up in front of the body 45 degrees below horizontal. Then the diver breaks into the slow run for the last 4 steps. When the diver takes the second step, he or she swings the arms on a straight line back behind the body approximately 1 foot. During the 3rd step the arms swing back to the same position as in the 1st step. During the 4th and 5th steps, the diver brings the arms back to the sides and laterally up to shoulder height as the hurdle begins, and the arms continue to move to the overhead position for the takeoff (see Figure 7.10, a-j). When practiced diligently, this run can also be done in a very rhythmic dancelike fashion, which adds a flair to the dive.

Whatever approach the diver chooses to perform, it should be smooth, flowing, and graceful, followed by a forceful, bold takeoff. Have the diver practice first on dry land, then on the pool deck, and then on the various platform levels. Practicing the running forward takeoff with a jump and an open-pike forward dive from the

Figure 7.10 Forward approach, 5-step run.

1-, 3-, and 5-meter levels is the best way for the diver to develop control of balance, rotational speed, and distance.

Running Reverse Takeoff

Although most divers prefer the standing reverse takeoff, there are some divers who use the running (walking) method. If the standing takeoff is not particularly effective for a given diver, the running method may be the answer.

One advantage of the running technique is that it provides a horizontal momentum prior to takeoff that may alleviate the fear of being too close, for divers who struggle with that problem.

In performing the running reverse takeoff, the diver, by rule, must take at least 4 steps. Therefore, a diver generally takes 4 or 5 steps, depending on which foot he or she wishes to push from in the takeoff. Even though the technical name of this approach is the running reverse, it is actually performed with walking steps, at a moderate speed.

If the diver uses a 4-step walk, the arms hang at the sides during the 1st step. In the 2nd step the arms stay parallel and swing forward to a position approximately 45 degrees below horizontal. During the 3rd step the arms are swung back behind the body, and in the last step the arms are swung forcefully forward and up to an overhead takeoff position. How far up and back overhead the arms move in the takeoff depends on the dive being done.

The difference between the 4- and 5-step approaches is that the arms hang at the sides during the first 2 steps of the 5-step method, then swing forward in step 3, backward in step 4, and forward and up into the takeoff in step 5.

The size of the steps should be a natural length for a medium speed of walk; however, the last step should be somewhat longer to allow for an increase in speed and force in preparation for the takeoff. You and the diver will have to experiment with various lengths of the last step to find a distance that looks good, is comfortable, and affords a strong jump from the platform.

The takeoff is performed from one foot, obviously the foot placed on the end of the platform after the 4th or 5th step. The takeoff foot is placed on the end of the platform with the heel first. Then as the foot rocks down on the sole of the foot, the hips and knee joints flex and the arms and other leg begin a swinging movement forward with the ankle extended. The arms remain straight, but the swinging leg bends so as not to drag across the surface of the platform. As the swinging arms and leg pass the drive leg, the diver rises up on the toes and extends the drive leg forcefully while the arms and swinging leg continue upward to help lift the diver into the air and help create whatever rotation is needed.

There are two methods of completing the lifting action of the swinging leg; the method used depends on the type of dive to be done. If the dive performed is in the straight or pike position, or is a reverse twisting dive, as the foot passes the edge of the platform, the diver straightens the knee and lifts the leg to a position as high as possible before the other foot leaves the platform. When the pushing leg does leave the platform, it is kept straight and lifted to bring the legs together, as quickly as possible. Figure 7.11, a-h, illustrates this type of takeoff.

Figure 7.11 Running reverse takeoff with straight leg.

When performing a tuck position dive, the diver keeps the swinging leg bent while lifting it up in front of the body. After the foot passes the edge of the platform, the diver lifts the thigh to approximately waist height while the knee bends to a 90-degree angle. When the drive leg leaves the platform, it is lifted alongside the other leg and flexed, as the arms come down from their overhead position and the diver performs a tuck. Figure 7.12, a-i, shows this method of takeoff.

a   b   c   d   e

f   g   h   i

Figure 7.12   Running reverse takeoff with bent leg.

Armstand (Handstand) Takeoff

The diver must first learn to balance and align a handstand on dry land or in a gymnasium. The diver can do this by practicing the handstand against a wall. The diver places the hands on the floor shoulder-width apart a few inches from the wall, with the back facing the wall. The diver then kicks up into the handstand by lifting one leg to the wall and then bringing the other leg up also, so both feet are against the wall at the start of the exercise. Then the diver moves the feet off the wall and balances the handstand. The diver should repeat this drill until he or she has a feel for the balance, and should then practice kicking up and holding the handstand without the wall. You can help the diver achieve a good body alignment by manually manipulating the hips and rib cage until a straight line in the back occurs.

When the diver can hold the handstand reasonably well, he or she can begin practice from the edge of the pool or a 1/2- or 1-meter platform. The diver must follow some basic points in performing this handstand.

- The hands should be positioned shoulder-width apart.
- The fingers should be spread and should overlap the edge of the takeoff surface by no more than the first or second joint of the middle three fingers.
- The shoulders should be directly over the edge of the takeoff surface before the kick-up starts.
- The eyes should focus on the edge of the takeoff surface between the hands.

Ultimately, the diver should learn to do a handstand "press." There are several variations of this skill, but basically a press means that the diver starts from a tuck or pike position, lifts the feet from the platform, shifts the balance totally to the hands, and then maneuvers the legs up to the armstand by whatever method is chosen.

Figures 7.13 through 7.15 show the most popular armstand press techniques: the tuck press, pike straddle press, and pike press.

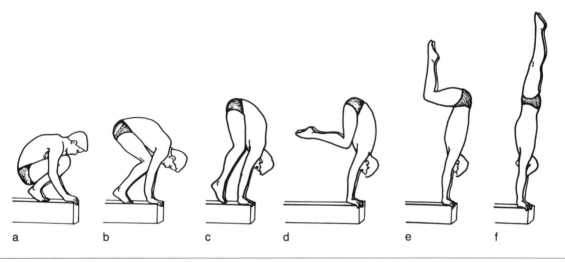

a   b   c   d   e   f

Figure 7.13   Armstand tuck press.

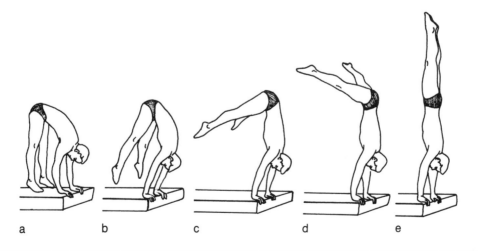

a   b   c   d   e

Figure 7.14   Armstand pike straddle press.

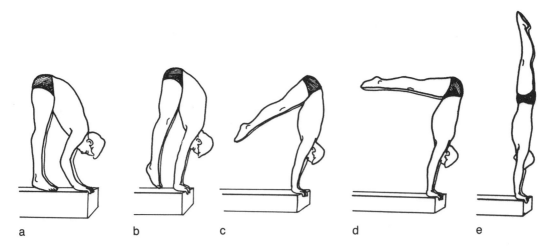

Figure 7.15 Armstand pike press.

When the diver learns the armstand—by kick-up or press method—so he or she has good balance and body line, it is time to learn the two directions of rotation that can be done from this takeoff. These will be presented in a later section of this chapter.

ENTRY DRILLS, LINEUPS, AND OPTIONAL COME-OUTS

The diver should continue to practice the takeoffs and various jumps described, to improve balance and control. At the same time training should begin on entry drills, lineups, and optional come-out techniques described in Chapter 2. A review of this section may be helpful, because the following sections will not explain those skills again but will merely refer to them. If a 3-meter platform is not available for the lineup drills to follow, the diver should practice them from a 3-meter springboard with the fulcrum in the most forward position to simulate the feeling of a platform.

Entry Drills

These drills consist of the standing forward hollow fall and standing backward fall. If a 3-meter platform level is available, this is the best place to practice these drills. Instruct the diver to do both the forward and backward falls with the arms first overhead in the entry position, and then in a lateral shoulder-high placement at the start and closing to the entry stretch during the fall-in.

When the diver can do these well at the 3-meter height, he or she can then move to the 5-meter platform and execute the same series of exercises. The eventual result should be entries that finish in a vertical path with proper body alignment, a flat-hand entry technique, the swimming motion of the arms underwater, and the appropriate somersault or backward knee save actions. If the diver achieves all these things and the entry path follows the ''go with the flow'' concept, a rip entry should occur.

Basic Dive Lineups

The basic forward, backward, reverse, and inward dive lineups are done with a lateral path of stretch for the entry. The diver should practice this type of lineup first and then add the optional come-out lineup.

Forward Lineups

The diver can perform these skills using five different starting positions: sitting roll-off, supported roll-off, standing fall, standing with spring, and running. Because we covered the sitting roll-off, standing open-pike fall, and standing-with-spring technique in the springboard lineup section, and because the running (forward approach) takeoff is self-explanatory, only the supported roll-off needs to be described.

The supported roll-off can only be done in the pike position. The diver sits with the legs straight and extending over the end of the platform from the knees. The diver places the hands palm down on the edge of the platform next to the legs and with the first two joints of the fingers curled around the edge. By straightening the arms, the diver lifts the body off the platform and supports the body on the hands while maintaining a pike position. The diver then shifts the weight forward with the upper body and rolls off the platform into an open-pike position with the arms moving to a straight and lateral placement at shoulder height as soon as the hands leave the platform.

The following list describes lineups the diver should practice, the order in which they should be practiced, as well as the various platform levels from which the diver can perform each skill. Keep in mind that all these lineups are done with a lateral path of stretch for the entry.

Lineup	Platform level
Standing open-pike fall	1, 3, 5, 7-1/2
Sitting open-pike roll-off	3, 5, 7-1/2
Sitting tuck roll-off	3, 5
Supported pike roll-off	3, 5, 7-1/2, 10
Standing open pike with spring	1, 3, 5
Standing tuck dive with spring	1, 3, 5
Running open pike	1, 3, 5

The running open-pike lineup exercise is particularly valuable because it not only affords lineup practice with a dive having more movement, but teaches the diver to jump strongly from the platform while maintaining control of rotation and distance. This is an absolutely essential skill in platform diving, especially if the diver later moves to the 7-1/2- and 10-meter heights. Because the supported pike roll-off is unique and is not illustrated in the springboard section, it is shown in Figure 7.16, a-e.

Inward Lineups

Because the inward and forward dive movements are so similar, the diver should learn inward lineups next. Unlike the forward lineups, inward lineups have only one starting position: the basic inward takeoff described previously. Also, only two dives can be done with inward lineups: the inward dive in open-pike position and the inward dive tuck. The diver should learn the open-pike dive first, because it is easier to control. Both these dives can be practiced from the 1-, 3-, and 5-meter heights.

Backward Lineups

There are five starting methods for these lineups: sitting roll-off, squatting roll-off, pop-up, standing fall, and standing with spring. All of these, except the pop-up technique, are described in the springboard presentation.

Figure 7.16   Supported forward pike roll-off from 5-meter height.

The pop-up is done with a small spring from a backward squatting position. The diver keeps the heels above the platform level and initiates the takeoff by dropping the heels to platform level and quickly extending the ankles while pulling upward on the legs, whether in a tuck or pike position. These movements, when coordinated, result in a hop-up or pop-up from the platform into the dive. This method gives the diver more of the feeling of the actual dive because of the spring involved and because the rotation of the dive occurs while the diver moves upward, instead of while the diver falls (as in the other takeoff methods).

Consult the following list to determine what skills the diver should practice, the learning progression, and the platform heights from which the diver should perform each skill. Again, the diver should use a lateral arm path to stretch for the entry.

Lineup	Platform level
Squat tuck roll-off	3, 5
Tuck pop-up	3, 5
Sitting tuck roll-off	3
Closed-pike pop-up	3

Standing closed-pike fall	5, 7-1/2
Closed-pike pop-up	5, 7-1/2
Sitting closed-pike roll-off	3
Standing backward dive tuck, with spring	3,5

The squat tuck roll-off, pop-up technique, and standing closed-pike fall are not illustrated in the springboard presentation, so they are shown in Figure 7.17, a-g, Figure 7.18, a-g, and Figure 7.19, a-e, respectively.

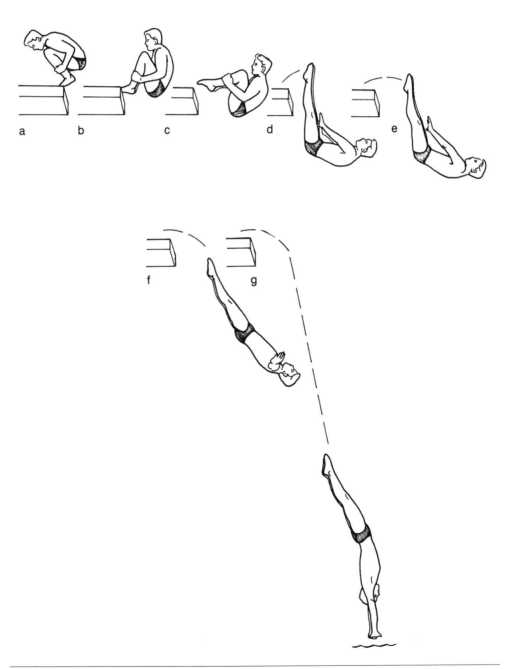

Figure 7.17 Backward squat tuck roll-off with lateral come-out from 5-meter height.

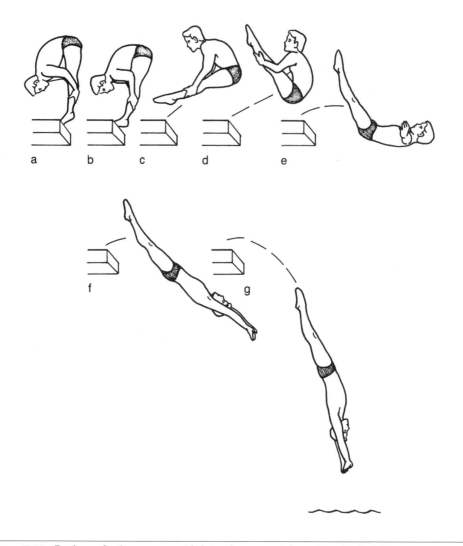

Figure 7.18   Backward pike pop-up with lateral come-out from 3-meter height.

Reverse Lineups

The diver performs this lineup from the standing reverse takeoff position by doing a reverse dive tuck with a lateral come-out. Even though the methods for practicing the reverse lineup are severely limited, practicing the various backward lineup exercises will have a strong carry-over effect, because the skills are very similar. If the diver develops good back entry technique and a good reverse takeoff action, he or she will be able to perform the reverse lineup very well.

Before the diver does the reverse dive tuck, practicing reverse jumps from the pool deck or 1-meter platform is helpful for developing balance and proper distance. When this is accomplished, the diver should practice the reverse dive tuck first from the 3-meter level and then from the 5-meter height.

Optional Come-Out Lineups

The choices for coming out of optional somersaulting dives are the same for platform and springboard dives. The diver can complete forward and inward optionals with the straight-line come-out if not much time is left before the entry, or with the pike-out method if time permits. The diver can finish backward and reverse optionals with the straight-line come-out for dives with little time for completion,

Figure 7.19 Backward closed-pike fall with lateral come-out from 5-meter height.

and with the grab-and-stretch method when there is sufficient time. For a more detailed description of these techniques, refer to chapter 4.

Forward Come-Out Lineups

These drills are done from the sitting roll-off starting position. The diver can practice the two types of come-out using the tuck roll-off and closed-pike roll-off drills.

The straight-line come-out in tuck and pike positions provides better training when done at the 3-meter height. Because this come-out is used in dives that allow the diver little time to prepare for the entry, the lower height of takeoff requires the diver to move more quickly and provides more effective practice. The pike-out technique, because it is used in dives with much more time before the entry, is best practiced at the 5- and 7-1/2-meter levels.

Inward Come-Out Lineups

The diver uses the basic inward takeoff action to start these skills and can practice them from deck level as well as from the 1-, 3-, and 5-meter platforms. The diver performs the inward dive tuck to practice the come-outs for this position. It's best for the diver to practice the straight-line technique at deck level and from 1- and 3-meter platforms, and the pike-out action at the 3- and 5-meter heights.

The diver can practice the pike position come-outs using a closed-pike inward dive for the straight-line come-outs at the recommended lower heights. However, due to the lack of time to get into and out of the pike position, most divers do not practice these drills, but transfer the movements learned from doing the tuck dives to the pike optionals. The inward dive in open-pike position, presented under basic dive lineups, serves as a practice method for the pike-out technique of completing inward pike optional dives.

Backward Come-Out Lineups

All five starting methods described under basic backward dive lineups can be used to practice these come-out skills: sitting roll-off, squatting roll-off, pop-up, standing fall pike, and standing with spring (backward dive tuck). You and the diver should experiment with all of these to determine which provides the best results. These lineups are usually confined to the 5-meter level and lower, although the closed-pike fall and pop-up takeoffs are sometimes done at the 7-1/2-meter level combined with the grab-and-stretch come-out action.

Here again, as much as your facilities allow, have the diver follow the guideline of doing the straight-line come-out at the lower levels and the grab-and-stretch movements at the higher heights. One particularly good drill for teaching divers to get into the straight-line stretch quickly, for the finish of the backward and reverse 1-1/2- and 2-1/2-somersault dives in tuck and pike positions, involves the diver performing the sitting tuck roll-off from a 2- to 2-1/2-foot-high bench placed on the 1-meter platform.

Reverse Come-Out Lineups

Like the inward come-outs, reverse come-outs offer limited choices for practice. The reverse dive tuck with standing reverse takeoff is the only skill available for this type of lineup. Performing the reverse dive tuck from the 3-meter platform with the straight-line come-out and from the 5-meter level with the grab-and-stretch action is the best training method. However, both the straight line and grab-and-stretch come-outs can be done at either the 3- or 5-meter height.

THE BASIC DIVES

After developing the fundamentals of the takeoffs, jumps, and lineups, which are the keys to effective platform diving, the diver is ready to learn the basic forward, backward, reverse, and inward dives in certain selected positions. Even though the diver may not use all of these in the actual program of competitive dives, they are essential to the diver's continuing development of good takeoff control, balance, and proper distance. The mechanics of execution are the same as those explained for springboard diving in chapter 3.

Forward Dive

This dive should be done in the pike position, because the dive allows the diver to jump up strongly in good distance. The forward dive straight, although a very good dive on the springboard, requires the diver to lean forward and dive away from the platform too much in order to clear the feet when passing platform level. Therefore, this dive does not encourage good takeoff technique.

The forward dive pike is done from the standing takeoff and should be performed first from the 3-meter platform, then taken to the 5-meter platform. If no 3-meter is available, the diver can easily do this dive from the 5-meter platform first.

Inward Dive

The diver can perform the inward dive in both the pike and straight positions; however, he or she should learn the pike position first. The diver should perform the inward dive in pike position from the 3-meter platform if that option is available, then from the 5-meter platform. The inward dive straight should be done from the 5-meter platform.

Whether the diver performs the inward dive straight, depends on choosing it as a dive to be done in competition. If it is not needed in the diver's program of competitive dives, then practicing the inward dive pike is sufficient.

Backward Dive

The diver should learn this dive in the pike position. The backward dive in straight position, like the forward dive straight, forces the diver to jump away from the platform to allow a safe clear distance with the feet as they pass platform level. This is not conducive to good takeoff technique, especially for the beginning diver. At a later stage of development, when takeoff mechanics are well established, the diver can try the backward dive in straight position, if necessary.

Before the diver does the backward dive pike, practicing a lead-up skill from the pool deck helps prepare the diver for better control of the takeoff. Instruct the diver to do the basic backward dive takeoff, jump up and back from the pool deck, then touch the toes and land on the seat in a pike position (see Figure 7.20, a-d).

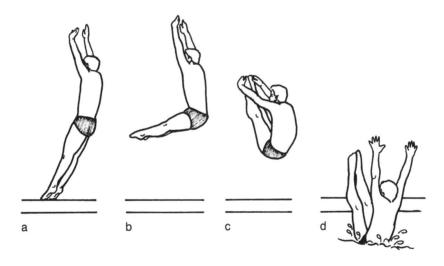

a   b   c   d

Figure 7.20   Backward dive pike lead-up skill.

Notice that the arms do not reach quite to a vertical line on takeoff (as they do with a springboard dive) and the diver touches the feet with the hands at approximately a 45-degree angle short of vertical. This angle of touch is done to control the amount of rotation. The diver should use the same technique in the actual backward dive pike from the platform. When the diver can do this lead-up drill with control, it is time to move to the platform.

If possible, the diver should execute this dive from the 3-meter level and perform it with an angle of entry short of vertical. When the diver does this well, he or she can move to the 5-meter platform.

Reverse Dive

The diver should learn the reverse dive in pike position first, because it better promotes the proper jump and distance from the platform. When the diver does this dive with good balance and distance, he or she can progress to the reverse dive straight.

Before performing the reverse dive pike, the diver should practice (from the side of the pool) the same type of lead-up skill that was used for the backward dive pike (see Figure 7.21, a-d). When the diver performs this drill with reasonable skill, he or she can do the reverse dive pike from the 5-meter platform. Because controlling rotation is much easier in this dive compared to the backward dive pike, it is not usually necessary to do this dive at the 3-meter level first.

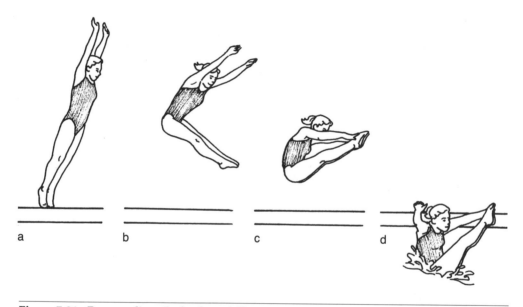

a   b   c   d

Figure 7.21 Reverse dive pike lead-up skill.

Before the diver does a reverse dive straight, practicing a reverse jump from the pool deck or 1-meter platform will serve as a good lead-up drill (review Figure 7.2). When the diver performs this skill with good balance and distance, the reverse dive straight should be done from the 5-meter platform.

THE OPTIONAL DIVES

With the exception of the armstand dives, which are covered in this section, the mechanics of execution for the optional dives are explained in the springboard presentation. Because the techniques used for optional springboard dives are the same in platform diving, we will not reiterate this material here. The important things to know about optional platform dives are what dives should be done at what level, and in what order the dives should be learned. The information on the effect of platform heights on various optional dives and lead-up skills is presented after the discussion of armstand dives, and the order in which the dives should be learned is covered in the next chapter.

Armstand Dives

Armstand dives can rotate in two directions on takeoff from the platform: forward and cut-through. From the armstand position, the forward dives begin with the body falling toward the water, and rotating in the same direction as forward dives. Cut-through dives begin with the diver moving the body away from the platform, while bringing the legs down through the space created between the front of the body and the edge of the platform. Cut-through dives rotate in the same direction as reverse dives.

Armstand (Forward) Somersault

This dive can be done in either the tuck or pike position. Usually when a diver does a somersault the entry is feetfirst, but because this dive begins in an inverted handstand position, a 360-degree rotation means the dive will enter headfirst.

The lead-up skill for this dive is an armstand forward fall to feet (1/2 somersault) from the 3-meter platform, or the 3-meter springboard if a platform is not available. The diver assumes the handstand position at the edge of the platform with the body and arms straight and the eyes fixed on the edge, between the hands. The diver falls toward the water, holding the straight alignment. It is especially important that the arms or hands do not move out of alignment, in order for the dive to stay on a straight somersault axis. The eyes should continue to focus on the platform edge during the fall. When the body has moved through approximately 20 degrees of fall, the diver moves to the tuck or pike position.

If the diver uses a tuck position, he or she draws the legs up toward the chest while the arms, head, and upper body move in a direct line toward the legs. The hands come directly over the top of the knees to grasp the lower legs at the midshin point, and the eyes sight over the top of the knees. Because only a 1/2-somersault rotation is being done, as soon as the diver assumes the tuck position, he or she must open immediately for a feetfirst entry (see Figure 7.22, a-e).

The diver should perform the same dive in pike position with the open-pike technique, due to the ease with which the dive can be controlled. At the same point in the fall as for the tuck position, the diver assumes the open pike by bending at the hips and moving the legs to the pike, while the head and upper body move toward the legs and the eyes sight the lower legs and feet. The diver keeps the arms straight and moves them from the platform in a lateral line to a shoulder-high open-pike position. As soon as this position is established, the diver must open from the pike for the feetfirst entry (see Figure 7.23, a-e).

When the diver does either of these lead-up dives satisfactorily, he or she may move to the 5-meter platform and continue rotation to the headfirst armstand somersault dive. The open-pike position requires a lateral close of the arms for the entry (see Figure 7.24, a-d).

However, the diver can do the tuck dive with either the straight-line come-out (which is recommended first) or the pike-out method. These dives are relatively easy to learn, but there are two common mistakes that can cause problems:

1. Bending the elbows during the fall
2. Moving to the tuck or pike position too early

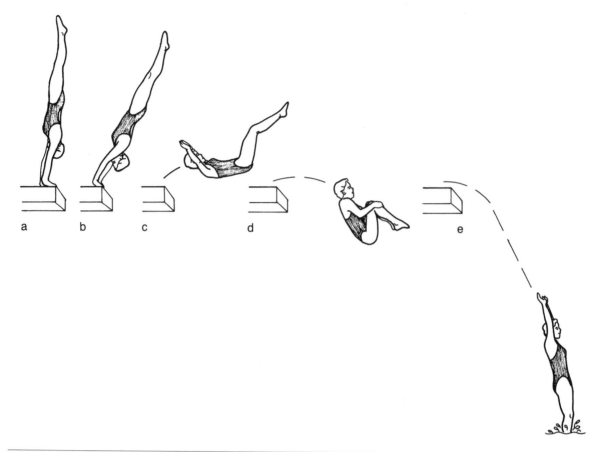

Figure 7.22   Armstand forward fall to feet in tuck position, from 3-meter height.

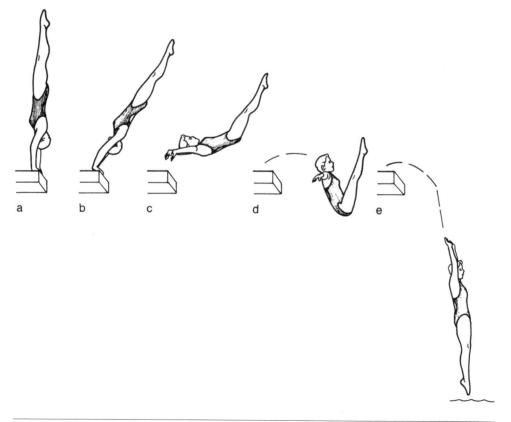

Figure 7.23   Armstand forward fall to feet in pike position, from 3-meter height.

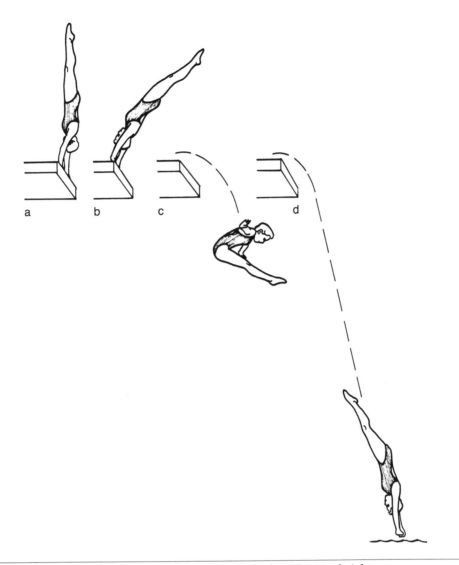

Figure 7.24 Armstand somersault in pike position, from 5-meter height.

Both of the errors cause a loss of rotation and bring the diver too close to the platform. Practice on the lead-up skill can alleviate both these faults.

Armstand Double Somersault

This dive is usually performed from the 7-1/2- or 10-meter height in the closed-pike position; however, some divers do execute it in the tuck position. Also, the diver should perform the armstand double somersault in tuck position from the 5- or 3-meter platform as a lead-up step to the armstand triple somersault from the 10-meter platform. The important basic skill, which will be explained here, is how to initiate rotation in order to complete the armstand double somersault, no matter what position or platform height is involved.

The lead-up skill the diver should practice here is the armstand somersault from the 3-meter platform; however, this skill can be done from the 5-meter level as long as the diver exhibits care not to overrotate. The starting position is the same as for the armstand somersault. The difference occurs during the falling phase of the takeoff, when the diver assumes a pike position at the instant the fall begins. How much pike occurs depends on the strength of the diver; however, the least amount of pike required to develop sufficient rotation is best. The deeper the pike becomes, the less aesthetic the takeoff becomes. At the end of the fall, the diver snaps the legs from the pike position and moves the body to a slight arch at the end of this movement. As the legs kick out of the pike, the shoulders and arms extend strongly against the platform to create a solid base for the rotational forces to develop. The actions and line of forces here are the same as for the forward rotating dives, described in chapter 5. Because the body is in an inverted position, the legs act as the arms and upper body, and the arms and hands act as the legs and feet. As soon as this pike–snap-out action is completed, the diver either tucks or pikes over to a headfirst entry (see Figure 7.25, a-g). Unlike the armstand somersault in pike position, the armstand double somersault requires the diver to move the arms in a straight line from the platform toward the legs, so the diver can establish a closed-pike position when doing the armstand double somersault.

With practice the diver will become proficient at creating a strong somersault rotation into the armstand somersault from the 3-meter platform. At this point, the diver can perform the armstand double somersault from either the 7-1/2- or 10-meter level.

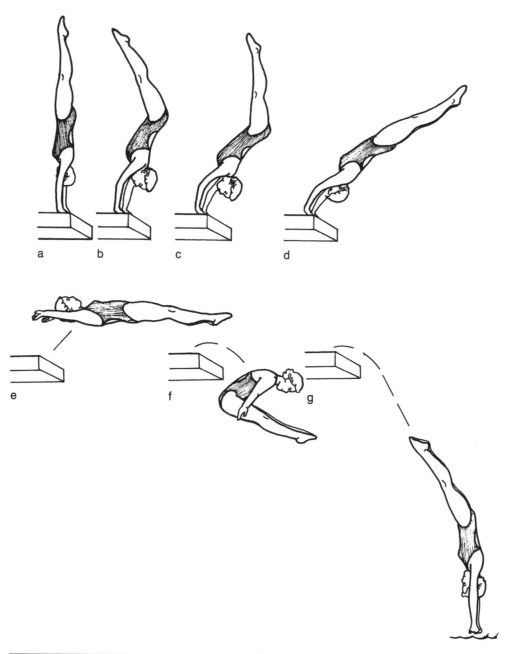

Figure 7.25 Armstand somersault in pike position, from 3-meter height.

Armstand Cut-Through

The other direction of rotation that can be initiated from the armstand takeoff is called *cut-through*. This term comes from the fact that the diver moves away from the platform while beginning rotation in the reverse somersaulting direction. The diver then brings the legs through the space created between the body and the platform. The term cut-through also indicates that the diver rotates to the feetfirst position; any designated amount of rotation in the reverse direction is calculated from this point. Therefore, to perform an armstand cut-through reverse dive, the diver performs an armstand cut-through to the feetfirst point of rotation and then continues rotating 1/2 somersault (reverse dive) to a headfirst entry. If doing an armstand cut-through reverse somersault, the dive continues rotating past the dive to a feetfirst entry.

To begin this type of dive, the diver needs to learn the simple armstand cut-through to the feetfirst entry from the 3- or 5-meter platform. The diver does this by beginning a fall in the same direction as for the armstand somersault, but with an arched body. The eyes focus on the platform edge between the hands during the takeoff. As soon as the diver reaches the ''point of no return'' where the body is out of balance forward, at approximately 10 to 15 degrees of fall, the diver reverses the direction of rotation by drawing the legs down to a tuck position while keeping the arms straight and pulling the arms against the platform in the direction of the body. This causes the diver to rotate through and past the platform to a feetfirst entry. As the movement to the tuck begins, the eyes shift their focus to the water (see Figure 7.26, a-e).

If performing this skill as an actual dive to be used in competition (which is rare), the diver should use a minimal amount of cut-through force in order to control the dive. When the move to the tuck position is completed, the body straightens and the arms move to a straight and lateral position at shoulder level. Just prior to the entry, the diver brings the arms laterally down to the side of the legs. If the diver is performing this dive strictly as a lead-up skill for the other cut-through dives, the amount of cut-through force will be much greater. So after the tuck is achieved and the body straightens, the arms can enter the water in an overhead position to help control rotation.

Armstand Cut-Through Reverse Dives

Three other dives can be done in the cut-through direction: armstand cut-through reverse dive, reverse somersault, and reverse 1-1/2 somersault. The diver usually learns the cut-through reverse dive first from the 7-1/2- or 10-meter platform, utilizing the fall and cut-through action described in the previous section. At a more advanced stage, the diver performs the armstand cut-through reverse dive in tuck position from the 5-meter height (see Figure 7.27, a-g), because it is an excellent lead-up skill for the cut-through reverse 1-1/2-somersault. The armstand cut-through reverse somersault is done from the 5-meter platform (see Figure 7.28, a-g), and is another lead-up skill for the cut-through reverse 1-1/2 somersault, which is performed from the 10-meter level.

The takeoff for the cut-through reverse dive and reverse somersault from the 5-meter and the cut-through 1-1/2 somersault from the 10-meter requires a stronger rotational force than can be generated with the fall and cut-through technique previously described. The diver can generate this strong rotational force by using a spring action from the handstand combined with a whiplike motion of the body. The diver can best practice this technique first on a tumbling mat and then from the edge of the pool or the 1-meter platform, before moving to the 5-meter height.

After the diver establishes the armstand balance, he or she begins a fall away from the platform accompanied by two other movements. The body changes from the straight alignment maintained in the handstand to an arch, and the shoulders drop from their elevated position over the ears in the handstand to their normal

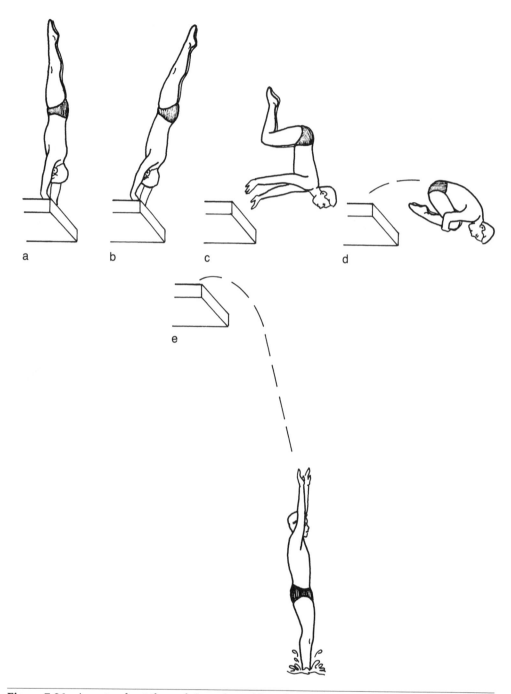

Figure 7.26   Armstand cut-through in tuck position, from 5-meter height.

level. After approximately 10 to 15 degrees of fall away from the platform, the diver simultaneously elevates the shoulders back up to the ears and snaps the body from the arch to a straight line. These movements, when timed correctly and coordinated, create reverse rotation. The diver then continues movement into either the tuck or pike position to accelerate the rotation and complete the dive being done. It is important that during the takeoff the diver keep the head still, and not tilt it back as many divers do. The diver can prevent head movement by shifting the eyesight from the edge of the platform to the water below and seeing the knees come into the tuck position, or the legs and feet come into the pike. This is the same visual technique as described for assuming these positions in backward and reverse somersaulting optionals.

When doing the cut-through reverse dive and reverse 1-1/2 somersault, the diver should use the visual spotting and come-out techniques described for the reverse somersaulting optionals in the springboard presentation.

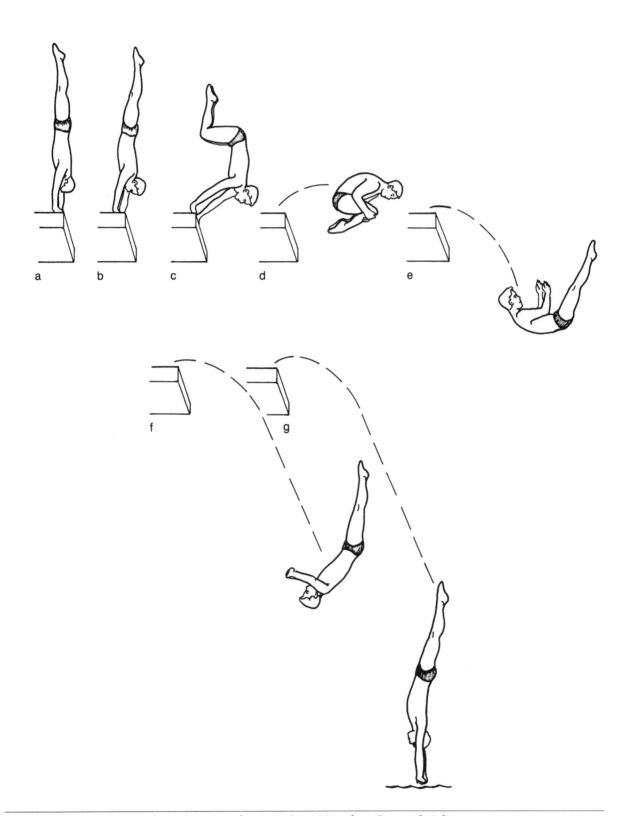

Figure 7.27   Armstand cut-through reverse dive in tuck position, from 5-meter height.

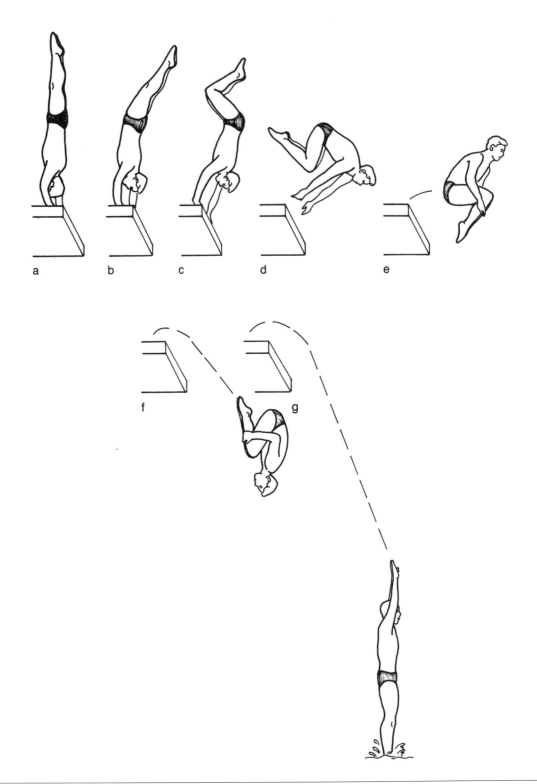

Figure 7.28   Armstand cut-through reverse somersault in tuck position, from 5-meter height.

WHAT DIVE, WHAT PLATFORM?

You need to know what optional dives and lead-up skills the diver can do from the 1-, 3-, and 5-meter platforms, so the diver does not attempt skills that are either unsafe or impossible. If the diver has established a good springboard background first and has worked sufficiently on the takeoffs, basic dives, and entries from the platform, performing most of the optional dives in the following list should be easy. Some of the more advanced optionals will require more time and training to master.

Core Skills

The optional dives to follow, combined with the takeoffs, jumps, line-ups, and basic dives plus the armstand somersault and armstand cut-through dives, form a group of core skills that every platform diver should learn at some time in his or her training. In the early stages of platform diving, the diver should practice these skills repeatedly in order to establish the correct pattern of movements, balance, and spatial orientation. As the diver becomes more advanced, whether he or she maintains all these skills in the training regimen depends on the program of dives being performed in competition.

The lists of dives presented here for the 1-, 3-, and 5-meter platform levels show the skills that should be practiced at these levels. The order in which they should be performed is discussed in chapter 8.

1 Meter

- Standing forward somersault tuck and pike
- Running forward somersault tuck and pike
- Running forward 1-1/2-somersault tuck and/or pike
- Backward somersault tuck and pike
- Reverse somersault tuck
- Inward somersault tuck

3 Meter

- Standing forward somersault tuck and pike
- Running forward somersault tuck and pike
- Running forward 1-1/2-somersault tuck and pike
- Backward somersault tuck, pike, and straight (hollow)
- Reverse somersault tuck and pike
- Inward somersault tuck and pike
- Inward 1-1/2-somersault tuck
- Forward somersault with 1 twist
- Backward somersault with 1/2 twist
- Backward somersault with 1-1/2 twists
- Armstand cut-through tuck
- Armstand 1/2-somersault (feetfirst) tuck and pike

5 Meter

- Standing forward 1-1/2-somersault tuck and pike
- Running forward 1-1/2-somersault tuck and pike
- Running forward 2-1/2-somersault tuck
- Backward somersault straight (hollow)
- Backward somersault tuck and pike
- Backward 1-1/2-somersault tuck and pike
- Reverse somersault tuck and pike
- Reverse 1-1/2-somersault tuck
- Inward 1-1/2-somersault tuck and pike
- Forward 1-1/2-somersault with 1 twist
- Backward 1-1/2-somersault with 1/2 twist
- Backward somersault with 1-1/2 twists
- Armstand cut-through tuck
- Armstand somersault tuck and pike

Lead-Up Skills

Although many of the core skills also serve as optional dives and lead-up skills, additional dives done from the 1-, 3-, and 5-meter platforms are specific lead-up steps for the more difficult optional dives at the 10-meter level. The diver may also use some of these dives as optional dives in competition from the 5-meter platform.

1 Meter

- Standing reverse somersault pike
- Inward 1-1/2-somersault tuck
- Armstand cut-through tuck
- Armstand somersault tuck

3 Meter

- Backward 1-1/2-somersault tuck
- Backward double somersault tuck
- Reverse 1-1/2-somersault tuck
- Reverse double somersault tuck
- Inward 1-1/2-somersault pike
- Forward somersault with 2 twists
- Backward somersault with 2-1/2 twists
- Armstand somersault tuck or pike
- Armstand double somersault tuck

5 Meter

- Running forward 2-1/2-somersault pike
- Running forward 3-1/2-somersault tuck
- Backward double somersault tuck and pike
- Backward 2-1/2-somersault tuck
- Reverse 1-1/2-somersault pike
- Reverse double somersault tuck and pike
- Reverse 2-1/2-somersault tuck
- Inward 2-1/2-somersault tuck
- Forward somersault with 3 twists
- Backward somersault with 2-1/2 twists
- Backward somersault with 3-1/2 twists
- Reverse somersault straight (hollow)
- Reverse somersault with 1-1/2 twists
- Reverse somersault with 2-1/2 twists
- Reverse somersault with 3-1/2 twists
- Armstand cut-through reverse dive tuck
- Armstand cut through reverse somersault tuck
- Armstand double somersault tuck

SUMMARY

Having covered the basic fundamentals of platform diving and the dives that can be done from the 1-, 3-, and 5-meter levels, we discuss in the next chapter how you and the diver can utilize these skills to develop a list of dives from the 7-1/2- and 10-meter platforms. Performing dives from these higher platforms will be safe and successful, if a sufficient amount of time and practice has been devoted to developing good control, balance, and spatial orientation in executing the fundamental skills covered in this chapter.

8
CHAPTER

DIVE AND SKILL PROGRESSIONS

In order to organize all the dives and skills discussed in the preceding chapters, you and the diver must develop a plan of diving progressions. This plan entails two distinct areas: the order in which the dives should be learned, or dive progressions, and the component skills within each dive, or skill progressions. When you and the diver know what dive to work on next, and the diver practices the essential parts of that dive before attempting it, you ensure a safe, logical, and successful transition from dive to dive.

GENERAL GUIDELINES

Before we specifically discuss dive and skill progressions, we need to cover some basic general guidelines that will help you make sound decisions when moving through the dive or skill progression process.

1. Have a plan to follow for both dive and skill progressions. Don't guess what comes next!
2. Evaluate the diver in three areas before allowing him or her to attempt a new dive or skill.
   a. Technique—The diver should possess good balance in the required take-off, consistently demonstrate safe distance from the board or platform, show sufficient spatial awareness in the lead-up skills, and possess proper mechanics of execution.
   b. Physical readiness—The diver should have sufficient strength and quickness to perform the dive or skill correctly and easily. Learning dives before he or she is physically ready causes the diver to use incorrect techniques, learn bad uncorrectable habits, and experience repeated failure in the performance. It is better to learn a dive too late than too soon.
   c. Mental readiness—The diver should demonstrate a level of confidence that indicates the ability to handle the stress of performing the dive or skill without panic and indicates a willingness to attempt the dive. Some

divers may have the techniques and physical abilities to do a dive but can't control their anxiety levels. When anxiety gets out of control, the diver may have unsafe balance and lack of control.

3. Ensure that the evaluation of the diver as presented above takes precedence over all other extraneous factors such as parents' wishes, diver's wishes, or requirements of an upcoming event.

4. Insist on correct performance of the preceding dive or skill before the diver moves to the next step. Most coaches and divers move too quickly through the dive and skill progressions for the diver to achieve high levels of execution along the way.

5. At the first sign that the dive or skill being done is too difficult or that technique is breaking down, return to the dive or skill level that the diver can perform successfully. Then return to the new dive when the diver is ready. Many times, regressing is progressing.

When you follow these guidelines and make wise decisions, the diver will develop confidence in his or her ability to do what you ask. The diver will know that when you say it is time to do a new dive or skill, he or she is well prepared and will perform it successfully and safely.

Patience and repetition of correct technique are the keys to smooth, safe, and successful progress!

DIVE PROGRESSION GUIDELINES

By following the guidelines presented here and referring to the skill progression charts found in this chapter, you can construct an appropriate plan of action for dive progressions. Keep in mind that the most important factors to consider are a logical progression of skills and the diver's safety and readiness for the skill.

Springboard Diving Progressions

As a general rule, in springboard diving the basic dives and somersaults are learned in this sequence: forward, backward, inward, reverse. The diver should learn these dives first in the tuck position, then in pike position, and finally in the straight position. Straight position somersaults are only done in the backward and reverse directions. The diver can learn the backward somersault straight in the early stages, but the reverse somersault straight is a more advanced dive and the diver should not learn it until preparing to learn reverse twisting dives or a reverse 1-1/2-somersault straight.

In learning the more difficult optional somersault and twisting dives, the diver should learn a dive in the forward direction before attempting it in the inward direction, and in the backward direction before the reverse direction. The exact learning sequence of forward/inward versus backward/reverse dives depends on the difficulty of the dive and the diver's technique and readiness to successfully execute it. For instance, most divers learn an inward 2-1/2-somersault tuck before doing a reverse 2-1/2-somersault tuck. However, this sequence may not be the best if the diver's inward technique is poor and he or she has good reverse takeoff action and good spatial awareness on backward and reverse spinning dives. You must carefully assess each diver's abilities in determining what dive to progress to next.

When progressing through the somersault dives in most situations, the diver will practice the dives in that direction (group) with 1 somersault rotation less and again with 1/2 somersault rotation less than the dive to be attempted, as lead-up skills. For example, if the diver is preparing for a forward 2-1/2-somersault pike from the 3-meter springboard, the lead-up skills he or she should practice from the 1-meter board are a forward 1-1/2-somersault pike, for come-out practice, and a forward double somersault pike, for takeoff and speed of somersault preparation.

Moving ahead on twisting dives follows the same general pattern. As lead-up skills, the diver performs the same number of somersaults with 1 less twist, and 1/2 less somersault rotation with the same number of twists as the new dive. For example, if the new dive to be performed is a forward 1-1/2-somersault with 2 twists from the 3-meter board, the lead-up skills would be a forward 1-1/2 somersault with 1 twist from the 1- and 3-meter levels, and a forward somersault with 2 twists from the 1-meter board.

One final guideline to follow when developing a dive progression plan is that the diver should learn a harder dive first on the 3-meter springboard before performing it on the 1-meter board. The reason for this recommendation is that the added time available at the 3-meter height allows the diver to execute this harder dive with correct technique. If the diver learns the dive first at the 1-meter level, the difficulty of completing the dive places tremendous pressure on the diver to force the dive and thereby use poor mechanics. Once the diver learns the new dive with incorrect actions and practices it repeatedly, changing those ingrained bad habits is extremely difficult.

In order to follow this recommendation, the diver must have a 3-meter springboard available and must learn to dive at that level. Unfortunately, many coaches and divers so not see the importance of using the 3-meter board, especially in the high school years because high school divers only compete at the 1-meter level. The door to learning the more difficult dives correctly on the 1-meter board is opened when the diver practices these dives first at the 3-meter height.

Platform Diving Progressions

Because most divers and coaches are less experienced in teaching platform diving and the order in which divers should learn dives and skills, a list of dive progressions for the dives covered in chapter 7 is presented here.

Lineup	Platform level
Standing reverse takeoff with jump	1, 3, 5
Backward takeoff with jump	1, 3, 5
Standing forward takeoff with jump	1, 3, 5
Inward takeoff with jump	1, 3, 5
Running forward takeoff with jump	1, 3, 5
Running reverse takeoff with jump	1
Standing forward hollow fall	3, 5
Backward fall (arms overhead)	3
Standing forward fall (lateral arms)	3, 5
Backward fall (arms lateral)	3
Forward lineup series	1, 3, 5
Inward lineup open pike	1, 3, 5

(Cont.)

Lineup	Platform level
Inward lineup tuck	1, 3, 5
Backward fall (arms overhead)	5
Backward fall (arms lateral)	5
Backward lineup series	3, 5
Reverse dive tuck	3, 5
Forward come-out lineups	3, 5
Inward come-out lineups	3, 5
Backward come-out lineups	3, 5
Reverse come-out lineups	3, 5
Standing forward dive pike	3, 5
Inward dive pike	3, 5
Backward dive pike	3, 5
Reverse dive pike	3, 5
Inward dive straight	5
Reverse dive straight	5
Armstand dive	1, 3
Armstand 1/2-somersault tuck and pike	3
Armstand cut-through	3, 5
Standing forward somersault tuck	1, 3
Standing forward somersault pike	3
Backward somersault tuck	1, 3, 5
Backward somersault pike	3, 5
Running forward somersault tuck	1, 3
Running forward somersault pike	1, 3
Running forward 1-1/2-somersault tuck	3
Running forward 1-1/2-somersault pike	3
Standing forward 1-1/2-somersault tuck	5
Standing forward 1-1/2-somersault pike	5
Running forward 1-1/2-somersault tuck	5
Running forward 1-1/2-somersault pike	5
Armstand somersault tuck and/or pike	5
Inward somersault tuck	1, 3

Lineup	Platform level
Inward 1-1/2-somersault tuck	5
Reverse somersault tuck	3, 5, 1
Running forward somersault open pike	3
Backward somersault straight (hollow)	3, 5
Running forward somersault with 1 twist	3
Running forward 1-1/2 somersault with 1 twist	5
Inward somersault pike	3
Inward 1-1/2-somersault pike	5
Backward 1-1/2-somersault tuck or pike	5
Running forward 1-1/2-somersault tuck	1
Running forward 2-1/2-somersault tuck	5
Reverse 1-1/2-somersault tuck	5
Backward somersault with 1-1/2 twists	3, 5

Using the chart on skill progressions in Table 8.2, you can study how these dives and skills fit into a plan for specific dives at all platform levels.

SKILL PROGRESSIONS

For any dive, several skills are combined to produce the overall result. When a diver segments a particular dive, learns and practices the component skills individually in a planned sequence, and then links those skills together in the execution of the dive, performance is optimized. The adage ''a chain is only as strong as its weakest link'' indicates the value of each skill or link to the ultimate level of execution of a dive. When a skill in any area of the dive is weak, that is the point where performance breaks down. A well-executed backward 3-1/2-somersault dive is merely an extension of a fundamentally sound single backward somersault with other skills added to it. If the diver doesn't have a good backward somersault technique, he or she either will not be able to perform a backward 3-1/2 somersault or will perform it poorly, no matter how much practice takes place.

To develop a logical and productive ''skill chain,'' you and the diver must know what skills are involved in each dive being executed, how these skills should be practiced, and in what sequence they should be practiced. The general skill areas that comprise dives are as follows:

1. Springboard or platform technique prior to the takeoff
2. Balance and angle of takeoff
3. Initiation of somersault rotation
4. Initiation of twist rotation
5. Spatial orientation
6. Come-out technique
7. Lineup and entry

You can help the diver isolate each of these components and gradually combine them as each part is executed correctly, through training on specific skills. Before discussing each of these skills I must point out the tremendous importance of correct body alignment to the success of each phase of the dive. If the diver does not constantly emphasize this foundation, the degree of expertise he or she develops in the skill chain is significantly reduced. You and the diver must pay attention to body alignment as each part of the dive is practiced.

Springboard or Platform Technique

The diver can best practice this phase of the dive by performing the appropriate board or platform work with a jump or tuck dive. These simpler skills allow the diver a high degree of concentration on the forward approach and backward take-off. Developing the ability to do a controlled, balanced jump or tuck dive with correct distance requires excellent skill in this area.

Balance and Angle of Takeoff

Performing the basic tuck dives in the various takeoff directions from the springboard and platform hones the skill required here. Also the forward and inward dives in open-pike position are helpful. These dives in the tuck and pike position require a high degree of accuracy, and mastering them will help the diver perform basic dives and optionals with good elevation and distance on takeoff.

Initiation of Somersault Rotation

Performing an easy somersaulting dive in the desired direction of rotation allows the diver to practice the correct movements needed to develop rotation but eliminates the pressure that accompanies a more difficult dive. Doing a forward 1-1/2 somersault or double in tuck position leads the diver into a more relaxed and successful forward 2-1/2 somersault, if the diver can start the harder 2-1/2-rotation dive with the same general pattern of movement as the easier dives. When the diver practices platform diving, executing a single standing somersault in the direction of rotation from the edge of the pool is also beneficial.

Initiation of Twist Rotation

The diver can also practice this most effectively by doing an easy twisting dive that is similar to the one for which he or she is training. This can be done in two steps. First the diver should perform a dive with the same number of somersaults but less twists, to practice the skills of somersaulting, twisting, and squaring out along with the completion of the dive. Next, the diver should perform a lead-up skill with the same number of twists desired, but with 1/2 less somersault, or a feetfirst entry.

Example: Dive to be done—Backward 1-1/2 somersault with 2-1/2 twists

Lead-up skills—Backward 1-1/2 somersault with 1-1/2 twists

Backward somersault with 2-1/2 twists

Spatial Orientation

The diver can best develop orientation for the whole dive by practicing the dive repeatedly on a trampoline or dry-land springboard with safety spotting equipment, and with a coach who is trained and knowledgeable in advanced spotting techniques. Whether this type of equipment and training are available or not, when attempting a new dive the diver must practice a dive with 1 somersault less rotation so he or she can concentrate on the proper angle of come-out when a somersault is added.

Let's use a backward 2-1/2 somersault as an example. The diver can develop spatial orientation for a backward 2-1/2 somersault from the springboard or platform by doing a backward 1-1/2 somersault from a lower level and concentrating on kicking out at the same approximate spot as desired when doing the 2-1/2 somersault. Another example would be doing the inward 1-1/2 somersault from the 1-meter board as preparation for the inward 2-1/2 somersault from the 3-meter height.

Come-Out Technique

The diver can train for this portion of the dive with three different skills: a lineup, a tuck or open-pike dive, and an easier dive in the same direction of rotation as the dive for which the diver is preparing. The less refined a diver's ability level, the more important it becomes to perform all three of these skills in preparation for the final dive.

Lineup and Entry

The diver can practice lineups and entries with the same three lead-up skills used for the come-out technique. It should be apparent that jumps, tuck dives, lineups, and easy optional dives are paramount to a skill-chain plan of preparation for a dive. As the diver becomes more and more proficient at the various skills in the chain, the amount of time he or she devotes to training for such skills may diminish. However, even the most skilled world-class divers should utilize this type of practice in the early stages of the training program, and at any time a particular dive, type of takeoff, or somersaulting or twisting skill deteriorates.

TRAINING GUIDELINES

In order to give you and the diver a road map to follow in the complicated development of skill chains for each particular dive, springboard and platform skills progression tables have been prepared. These list the dives, corresponding lead-up skills at the various heights of springboard and platform, and their order of performance. Locate the dive and height for which the diver is preparing, and you'll find the links of the chain leading to it listed below in the numerical order of execution. In the case of platform dives, if your training facility does not have the recommended platform height for the skill indicated, you will have to eliminate that skill from the preparation and training process or have the diver practice the skill on the springboard.

I hope that these skill progression guides for springboard and platform dives will aid you and your divers in training more effectively for better performance. You can use these progressions in two distinct ways within the training program.

Individual Skill Training Program

With this type of program, the diver will work on each of the skills leading to the ultimate dive, performing a high number of repetitions on each skill before progressing to the next skill. It is very possible that the diver will devote an entire practice or several practices to one particular skill, because it is the weakest link in the chain. The diver may have to further break down individual skills into component parts and train for each part first, either in the dry-land or pool setting, before combining the parts into the whole performance.

Progressive Skill Training Program

After the diver has used the individual skill training process to practice and master each of the skills in the chain leading toward a particular dive, these parts can be put together more rapidly. The diver does this by performing each skill in order, doing only the minimum number of repetitions of each necessary to achieve a good execution, then moving to the next skill.

Example: Dive to be done—Forward 2-1/2-somersault tuck from the 1-meter springboard.

Skill 1—Forward approach and front jump from 1-meter level

Skill 2—Forward dive tuck with straight-line come-out from 1-meter level

Skill 3—Forward 1-1/2 somersault tuck from 1-meter level

Skill 4—Forward tuck roll-off with straight-line come-out from 3-meter level

The diver then performs the forward 2-1/2-somersault tuck a few times. If the results are good, the diver moves to another dive, but if not the diver repeats the progressive skill process. You and the diver decide how many times this skill chain is done.

Using the Charts

The dives on the skill progression charts are listed by dive number and body position as contained in the official diving table for competition (see Table 8.1). The skill progressions begin with the assumption that the diver has learned the basic dives and single somersault dives in all four directions, so progressions for these skills are not included. Also, dives that are rarely performed and dives that are not recommended because they do not lead to a suitable competitive dive have been omitted from the charts.

The dives to be done at the highest height possible, 3 meters for springboard and 10 meters for platform, are listed horizontally across the top of the chart (see Tables 8.2 and 8.3). The skill progression for the particular dive selected is shown vertically under the dive number with the recommended numerical order in which the skills should be performed. To determine the skill progression for a dive at any other height, locate the dive number at the appropriate level (1, 3, 5, or 7.5 meters) on the left side of the table for that group, and follow it across the table to the first column with a number in it. All the progressions leading to that dive are listed numerically below that point. The springboard table contains a separate progression for the 3-meter and 1-meter heights.

Additionally, following are some clarifications on performance of specific skills and unusual situations that may occur.

1. You or the diver needs to evaluate the diver's ability to perform each skill progression before he or she performs it. The 107C, which is listed at the 7.5-meter platform level as a progression toward that dive on the 10-meter level, is to be done by divers who spin unusually fast and may have control problems in their first few attempts at the 10-meter height. Most divers will not somersault fast enough to do the 3-1/2 somersault at 7.5 meters and should move from the 105C at 5 meters to the 107C at the 10-meter level. Or the opposite situation may occur; the diver may not spin fast enough to do a recommended progression. For example, in the 305C platform progres-

sion, many divers may not be able to make the 305C at the 7.5-meter level. In this case the diver should progress from the 304C at 5 meters to 305C at 10 meters.

2. When the same skill progression number occurs at two different platform levels, you need to make a decision, based on the diver's skills, whether he or she should do the progression from both heights or only one level. These dual numbers also account for facilities in which all levels of platform are not available.

3. Whenever a platform height is not available for a skill progression, and also as a complement to the progression process, the diver can utilize the 1- and 3-meter springboards to learn and practice platform dives.

4. Where a lineup is indicated on the chart, you and the diver should select the lineup and come-out method that best fits the dive being done.

5. When the diver performs the 104B progression listed for the 5152 and 5154 dives from the springboard, the diver should move from the pike position to straight position at the 1-1/2-somersault point and remain straight for the completion of the dive. This lead-up skill will orient the diver as to when to come out of the somersault into the twist, in the actual dives.

6. Where 202A or 302A dives are shown, the diver should perform these in the hollow straight position, as described in chapter 6.

7. There are two abbreviations on the charts:
   S = standing takeoff
   OP = open-pike position

What Dive to Use?

As the diver learns new dives in each of the groups, the question always arises, What dive should I use in competition? Should the diver perform the higher degree of difficulty dive, which will probably result in lower judges' scores, or the lower degree of difficulty, which may net higher judges' scores? Here's a good general rule to solve this dilemma: Determine what the average expected judges' scores would be for each of these dives if they were performed in competition several times. Next apply this formula: ±.2 degree of difficulty is equal to ±.5 points in judges' scores.

Example: 2.2 degree of difficulty × 7-point judges' scores =

3.6 degree of difficulty × 6-point judges' scores =

3.0 degree of difficulty × 5-point judges' scores =

This simple calculation can give you a quick basis on which to decide what dive to use. Because total point score, not degree of difficulty, is the determining factor in place finish, the dive to use should be obvious. If the net result for the two dives is similar, the diver should use the higher degree of difficulty dive providing the diver's technique is fundamentally sound.

One other point to keep in mind is that in high-pressure meets (championships), the stress involved brings out flaws in the mechanics of dives and can result in poor execution. In these circumstances, the diver should select the dive that is most technically correct.

SUMMARY

I hope this chapter will help you take all the technical information from the other chapters and put it together into a well-planned and well-thought-out training program. With a precise direction, correct step-by-step practice, and some wise decision making along the way, remarkable progress is sure to occur.

The principles and guidelines presented here are only a framework for you and your diver to use. It is important that you continually use imagination and inventiveness to improve upon and add to the learning process. Experimentation and trial and error are the cornerstones of progress. Without the willingness of you and your diver to utilize these tools to find better ways, our teaching and learning skills will stagnate, so be creative in your approach to diving.

Table 8.1   FINA Table of Degree of Difficulties

SPRINGBOARD		1 METER				3 METER			
		Strt	Pike	Tuck	Free	Strt	Pike	Tuck	Free
	FORWARD GROUP	A	B	C	D	A	B	C	D
001	Forward Entry								1.0
100	Forward Jump	1.0	1.0	1.0		1.0	1.0	1.0	
101	Forward Dive	1.4	1.3	1.2		1.6	1.5	1.4	
102	Forward Somersault	1.6	1.5	1.4		1.7	1.6	1.5	
103	Forward 1-1/2 Somersault		1.7	1.6		1.9	1.6	1.5	
104	Forward Double Somersault		2.3	2.2			2.1	2.0	
105	Forward 2-1/2 Somersault		2.6	2.4			2.4	2.2	
106	Forward Triple Somersault			2.9				2.5	
107	Forward 3-1/2 Somersault			3.0			3.1	2.8	
109	Forward 4-1/2 Somersault							3.5	
112	Forward Flying Somersault		1.7	1.6			1.8	1.7	
113	Forward Flying 1-1/2 Somersault		1.9	1.8			1.8	1.7	
114	Forward Flying Double Somersault								
115	Forward Flying 2-1/2 Somersault							2.5	
1051	Forward Somersault with Flying 1-1/2 Somersault							2.5	
	BACKWARD GROUP	A	B	C	D	A	B	C	D
002	Back Entry								1.0
200	Back Jump	1.0	1.0	1.0		1.0	1.0	1.0	
201	Back Dive	1.7	1.6	1.5		1.9	1.8	1.7	
202	Back Somersault	1.7	1.6	1.5		1.8	1.7	1.6	
203	Back 1-1/2 Somersault	2.5	2.4	2.0		2.4	2.2	1.9	
204	Back Double Somersault		2.5	2.2		2.5	2.3	2.0	
205	Back 2-1/2 Somersault		3.2	3.0			3.0	2.8	
207	Back 3-1/2 Somersault							3.4	
212	Back Flying Somersault		1.7	1.6			1.8	1.7	
213	Back Flying 1-1/2 Somersault							2.1	
	REVERSE GROUP	A	B	C	D	A	B	C	D
301	Reverse Dive	1.8	1.7	1.6		2.0	1.9	1.8	
302	Reverse Somersault	1.8	1.7	1.6		1.9	1.8	1.7	
303	Reverse 1-1/2 Somersault	2.7	2.4	2.1		2.6	2.3	2.0	
304	Reverse Double Somersault		2.6	2.3			2.4	2.1	
305	Reverse 2-1/2 Somersault		3.2	3.0			3.0	2.8	
307	Reverse 3-1/2 Somersault							3.5	
312	Reverse Flying Somersault		1.8	1.7				1.8	
313	Reverse Flying 1-1/2 Somersault							2.2	
	INWARD GROUP	A	B	C	D	A	B	C	D
401	Inward Dive	1.8	1.5	1.4		1.7	1.4	1.3	
402	Inward Somersault		1.7	1.6			1.5	1.4	
403	Inward 1-1/2 Somersault		2.4	2.2			2.1	1.9	

(Cont.)

Table 8.1 (Continued)

SPRINGBOARD		1 METER				3 METER			
		Strt	Pike	Tuck	Free	Strt	Pike	Tuck	Free
INWARD GROUP (Cont.)		A	B	C	D	A	B	C	D
404	Inward Double Somersault			2.6			2.6	2.4	
405	Inward 2-1/2 Somersault		3.4	3.0			3.0	2.7	
407	Inward 3-1/2 Somersault							3.4	
412	Inward Flying Somersault		2.1	2.0			1.9	1.8	
413	Inward Flying 1-1/2 Somersault			2.7				2.4	
FRONT TWISTING GROUP		A	B	C	D	A	B	C	D
5111	Forward Dive 1/2 Twist	1.8	1.7			2.0	1.9		
5112	Forward Dive 1 Twist	2.0	1.9			2.2	2.1		
5121	Forward Somersault 1/2 Twist	1.9	1.8		1.7	2.0	1.9		
5122	Forward Somersault 1 Twist				1.9				2.0
5124	Forward Somersault 2 Twists				2.3				
5126	Forward Somersault 3 Twists				2.7				
5131	Forward 1-1/2 Somersault 1/2 Twist		2.1	2.0			2.0	1.9	
5132	Forward 1-1/2 Somersault 1 Twist				2.2				2.1
5134	Forward 1-1/2 Somersault 2 Twists				2.6				2.5
5136	Forward 1-1/2 Somersault 3 Twists				3.0				2.9
5138	Forward 1-1/2 Somersault 4 Twists								3.3
5152	Forward 2-1/2 Somersault 1 Twist				3.0				2.8
5154	Forward 2-1/2 Somersault 2 Twists								3.2
BACK TWISTING GROUP		A	B	C	D	A	B	C	D
5211	Back Dive 1/2 Twist	1.8				2.0			
5212	Back Dive 1 Twist	2.0				2.2			
5221	Back Somersault 1/2 Twist				1.7				
5222	Back Somersault 1 Twist				1.9				
5223	Back Somersault 1-1/2 Twists				2.3				
5225	Back Somersault 2-1/2 Twists				2.7				
5231	Back 1-1/2 Somersault 1/2 Twist				2.1				2.0
5233	Back 1-1/2 Somersault 1-1/2 Twists				2.5				2.4
5235	Back 1-1/2 Somersault 2-1/2 Twists				2.9				2.8
5237	Back 1-1/2 Somersault 3-1/2 Twists								3.2
5251	Back 2-1/2 Somersault 1/2 Twist								2.5
REVERSE TWISTING GROUP		A	B	C	D	A	B	C	D
5311	Reverse Dive 1/2 Twist	1.9				2.0			
5312	Reverse Dive 1 Twist	2.1				2.2			
5321	Reverse Somersault 1/2 Twist				1.8				
5322	Reverse Somersault 1 Twist				2.0				
5323	Reverse Somersault 1-1/2 Twists				2.4				
5325	Reverse Somersault 2-1/2 Twists				2.8				
5331	Reverse 1-1/2 Somersault 1/2 Twist				2.2				2.1

Table 8.1   (Continued)

SPRINGBOARD		1 METER				3 METER			
		Strt	Pike	Tuck	Free	Strt	Pike	Tuck	Free
REVERSE TWISTING GROUP (Cont.)		A	B	C	D	A	B	C	D
5333	Reverse 1-1/2 Somersault 1-1/2 Twists				2.6				2.5
5335	Reverse 1-1/2 Somersault 2-1/2 Twists				3.0				2.9
5337	Reverse 1-1/2 Somersault 3-1/2 Twists								3.3
5351	Reverse 2-1/2 Somersault 1/2 Twist								2.5
INWARD TWISTING GROUP		A	B	C	D	A	B	C	D
5411	Inward Dive 1/2 Twist	2.0	1.7			1.9	1.6		
5412	Inward Dive 1 Twist	2.2	1.9			2.1	1.8		
5421	Inward Somersault 1/2 Twist			1.8	1.7		1.6	1.5	
5422	Inward Somersault 1 Twist				2.1				
5432	Inward 1-1/2 Somersault 1 Twist				2.7				2.4
5434	Inward 1-1/2 Somersault 2 Twists				3.1				2.8

PLATFORM		10 METERS				7.5 METERS				5 METERS			
		Strt	Pike	Tuck	Free	Strt	Pike	Tuck	Free	Strt	Pike	Tuck	Free
FORWARD GROUP		A	B	C	D	A	B	C	D	A	B	C	D
101	Forward Dive	1.6	1.5	1.4		1.6	1.5	1.4		1.4	1.3	1.2	
102	Forward Somersault	1.8	1.7	1.6		1.7	1.6	1.5		1.6	1.5	1.4	
103	Forward 1-1/2 Somersault	1.9	1.6	1.5		1.9	1.6	1.5		2.0	1.7	1.6	
104	Forward Double Somersault	2.5	2.2	2.1			2.1	2.0			2.3	2.2	
105	Forward 2-1/2 Somersault		2.3	2.1			2.4	2.2			2.6	2.4	
106	Forward Triple Somersault												
107	Forward 3-1/2 Somersault		3.0	2.7				2.8				3.0	
109	Forward 4-1/2 Somersault			3.5									
112	Forward Flying Somersault		1.9	1.8			1.8	1.7			1.7	1.6	
113	Forward Flying 1-1/2 Somersault		1.8	1.7			1.8	1.7			1.9	1.8	
114	Forward Flying Double Somersault			2.3				2.2					
115	Forward Flying 2-1/2 Somersault		2.6	2.4				2.5					
1051	Forward Somersault with Flying 1-1/2 Somersault			2.4				2.5					

PLATFORM		10 METERS				7.5 METERS				5 METERS			
		Strt	Pike	Tuck	Free	Strt	Pike	Tuck	Free	Strt	Pike	Tuck	Free
BACKWARD GROUP		A	B	C	D	A	B	C	D	A	B	C	D
201	Back Dive	1.9	1.8	1.7		1.9	1.8	1.7		1.7	1.6	1.5	
202	Back Somersault	1.9	1.8	1.7		1.8	1.7	1.6		1.7	1.6	1.5	
203	Back 1-1/2 Somersault	2.4	2.2	1.9		2.4	2.2	1.9		2.5	2.4	2.0	
204	Back Double Somersault	2.6	2.4	2.1		2.5	2.3	2.0			2.5	2.2	
205	Back 2-1/2 Somersault	3.3	2.9	2.7			3.0	2.8				3.0	
207	Back 3-1/2 Somersault			3.3				3.4					
212	Back Flying Somersault		1.9	1.8			1.8	1.7			1.7	1.6	
213	Back Flying 1-1/2 Somersault			2.1				2.1					

(Cont.)

Table 8.1   (Continued)

	PLATFORM	10 METERS				7.5 METERS				5 METERS			
		Strt	Pike	Tuck	Free	Strt	Pike	Tuck	Free	Strt	Pike	Tuck	Free
	REVERSE GROUP	A	B	C	D	A	B	C	D	A	B	C	D
301	Reverse Dive	2.0	1.9	1.8		2.0	1.9	1.8		1.8	1.7	1.6	
302	Reverse Somersault	2.0	1.9	1.8		1.9	1.8	1.7		1.8	1.7	1.6	
303	Reverse 1-1/2 Somersault	2.6	2.3	2.0		2.6	2.3	2.0		2.7	2.4	2.1	
304	Reverse Double Somersault		2.5	2.2			2.4	2.1			2.6	2.3	
305	Reverse 2-1/2 Somersault		2.9	2.7			3.0	2.8				3.0	
307	Reverse 3-1/2 Somersault			3.4									
312	Reverse Flying Somersault			1.9				1.8			1.8	1.7	
313	Reverse Flying 1-1/2 Somersault			2.2				2.2					
	INWARD GROUP	A	B	C	D	A	B	C	D	A	B	C	D
401	Inward Dive	1.7	1.4	1.3		1.7	1.4	1.3		1.8	1.5	1.4	
402	Inward Somersault		1.6	1.5			1.5	1.4			1.7	1.6	
403	Inward 1-1/2 Somersault		2.0	1.8			2.1	1.9			2.4	2.2	
404	Inward Double Somersault		2.6	2.4			2.6	2.4				2.6	
405	Inward 2-1/2 Somersault		2.8	2.5			3.0	2.7				3.0	
407	Inward 3-1/2 Somersault		3.5	3.2				3.4					
412	Inward Flying Somersault		2.0	1.9			1.9	1.8				2.0	
413	Inward Flying 1-1/2 Somersault		2.5	2.3				2.4					
	FRONT TWISTING GROUP	A	B	C	D	A	B	C	D	A	B	C	D
5111	Forward Dive 1/2 Twist	2.0	1.9			2.0	1.9			1.8	1.7		
5112	Forward Dive 1 Twist	2.2	2.1			2.2	2.1			2.0	1.9		
5121	Forward Somersault 1/2 Twist					2.0	1.9			1.9	1.8		1.7
5122	Forward Somersault 1 Twist												1.9
5124	Forward Somersault 2 Twists												2.3
5126	Forward Somersault 3 Twists												
5131	Forward 1-1/2 Somersault 1/2 Twist										2.1	2.0	
5132	Forward 1-1/2 Somersault 1 Twist				2.1				2.1				2.2
5134	Forward 1-1/2 Somersault 2 Twists				2.5				2.5				2.6
5136	Forward 1-1/2 Somersault 3 Twists				2.9				2.9				
5138	Forward 1-1/2 Somersault 4 Twists				3.3				3.3				
5152	Forward 2-1/2 Somersault 1 Twist				2.7								
5154	Forward 2-1/2 Somersault 2 Twists				3.1				3.2				
	BACK TWISTING GROUP	A	B	C		A	B	C		A	B	C	D
5211	Back Dive 1/2 Twist	2.0				2.0				1.8			
5212	Back Dive 1 Twist	2.2				2.2				2.0			
5221	Back Somersault 1/2 Twist												1.7
5222	Back Somersault 1 Twist												1.9
5223	Back Somersault 1-1/2 Twists												2.3
5225	Back Somersault 2-1/2 Twists												2.7
5231	Back 1-1/2 Somersault 1/2 Twist				2.1				2.0				2.1

Table 8.1   (Continued)

PLATFORM	10 METERS Strt (A)	Pike (B)	Tuck (C)	Free (D)	7.5 METERS Strt (A)	Pike (B)	Tuck (C)	Free (D)	5 METERS Strt (A)	Pike (B)	Tuck (C)	Free (D)
BACK TWISTING GROUP (Cont.)	A	B	C	D	A	B	C	D	A	B	C	D
5233 Back 1-1/2 Somersault 1-1/2 Twists				2.4				2.4				2.5
5235 Back 1-1/2 Somersault 2-1/2 Twists				2.8				2.8				
5237 Back 1-1/2 Somersault 3-1/2 Twists				3.2								
5251 Back 2-1/2 Somersault 1/2 Twist				2.4				2.4				
REVERSE TWISTING GROUP	A	B	C	D	A	B	C	D	A	B	C	D
5311 Reverse Dive 1/2 Twist	2.0				2.0				1.9			
5312 Reverse Dive 1 Twist	2.2				2.2				2.1			
5321 Reverse Somersault 1/2 Twist												1.8
5322 Reverse Somersault 1 Twist												2.0
5323 Reverse Somersault 1-1/2 Twists												2.4
5325 Reverse Somersault 2-1/2 Twists												2.8
5331 Reverse 1-1/2 Somersault 1/2 Twist				2.1				2.1				2.2
5333 Reverse 1-1/2 Somersault 1-1/2 Twists				2.5				2.5				2.6
5335 Reverse 1-1/2 Somersault 2-1/2 Twists				2.9				2.9				
5337 Reverse 1-1/2 Somersault 3-1/2 Twists				3.3								
5351 Reverse 2-1/2 Somersault 1/2 Twist				2.4								
INWARD TWISTING GROUP	A	B	C	D	A	B	C	D	A	B	C	D
5411 Inward Dive 1/2 Twist	1.8	1.5			1.9	1.6			2.0	1.7		
5412 Inward Dive 1 Twist	2.0	1.7			2.1	1.8			2.2	1.9		
5421 Inward Somersault 1/2 Twist			1.7	1.6			1.6	1.5			1.8	1.7
5422 Inward Somersault 1 Twist												
5432 Inward 1-1/2 Somersault 1 Twist				2.3				2.4				2.1
5434 Inward 1-1/2 Somersault 2 Twists				2.7								
ARMSTAND GROUP	A	B	C	D	A	B	C	D	A	B	C	D
600 Armstand Dive	1.6				1.6				1.5			
611 Armstand Back Fall	2.0				2.0				1.8			
612 Armstand Somersault	2.0	1.9	1.7		1.9	1.8	1.6		1.8	1.7	1.5	
614 Armstand Double Somersault		2.4	2.1			2.3	2.0				2.2	
616 Armstand Triple Somersault		2.8										
631 Armstand Forward Cut-through	1.9	1.8	1.6		1.9	1.8	1.6			1.6	1.4	
632 Armstand Cut-through Reverse Dive		2.3	2.1			2.2	2.0				1.9	
633 Armstand Cut-through Reverse Somersault			2.0				2.0				2.1	
634 Armstand Cut-through Reverse 1-1/2 Somersault			2.6				2.5					

Note. Table 8.1 from *United States Diving Rules and Regulations* (pp. 106-109) by United States Diving, Inc., 1991, Indianapolis, IN: Author. Copyright 1991 by United States Diving, Inc. Reprinted by permission.

Table 8.2 Springboard Skill Progressions

GROUP I - FORWARD

3M	103C	103B	105C	105B	107C	107B	109C
Line-up	4	4	5	5	4		
1M							
107C							3
105B						3	
105C					3		2
104B				4			
104C			4				
103B				3		2	
103C			3		2		
102B		3					
102C	3						
101C	2	2	2	2	1	1	1
Jump	1	1	1	1			

1M	103C	103B	104C	104B	105C	105B	107C
105C							3
104C				4			
103B					3	3	
103C			3		3		2
102B		3					
102C	3						
101C	2	2	2	2	2	2	1
Jump	1	1	1	1	1	1	
3M							
Line-up	4	4			5	4	

GROUP II - BACKWARD

3M	203C	203B	203A	205C	205B
Line-up	4	4	3	5	5
1M					
204B					4
204C				4	
203B					3
203C				3	
202A			2		
202B		3			
202C	3				
201C	2	2		2	2
Jump	1	1	1	1	1

1M	203C	203B	203A	205C
204C				2
202A		3		
202B		3		
202C	3			
201C	2	2	2	1
Jump	1	1	1	
3M				
Line-up	4	4	4	3

GROUP III - REVERSE

3M	303C	303B	303A	305C	305B
1M					
304B					3
304C				3	
303B					2
303C				2	
302A			3		
302B		3			
302C	3				
301C	2	2	2	1	1
Jump	1	1	1		

1M	303C	303B	303A	305C
304C				1
302A			2	
302B		2		
302C	2			
301C	3	3	3	2
Jump	1	1	1	

GROUP IV - INWARD

3M	403C	403B	404C	405C	405B
Line-up					1
1M					
403B					4
403C			3	4	
402B		2			
402C	2				
401C	3	3	2	3	3
Jump	1	1	1	2	2

1M	403C	403B	405C
403C		2	
402B		3	
402C	3		
401C	2	2	1
Jump	1	1	
3M			
403B		4	

Table 8.2 (Continued)

3M	5132	5134	5136	5231	5233	5235	5237	5331	5333	5335	5337	5152 in out	5154 in out
						GROUP Va - TWISTING							
Line-up	4			4	4								
5132		4											
5134			3										
5233						4							
5235							3						
5333										4			
5335											3		
5152													3
1M													
5126			4										
5124		5	2										
5122	3	3											
102B	2	2	1										
5227							4						
5225						5	2						
5223					3	3							
5221				3									
202A				2	2	2	1						
5327										5	4		
5325											2		
5323									3	3			
5321								3					
302A								2	2	2	1		
5144													4
5142												2	2
5134													
5132												2	
104B												1	1
103B (OP)												1	1
Jump	1	1		1	1	1		1	1	1			

(Cont.)

Table 8.2   (Continued)

					GROUP Vb - TWISTING										
1M	5122	5132	5124	5134	5136	5231	5223	5233	5225	5235	5331	5333	5335	5152 (in)
5126					3									
5134					2									
5124														
5132				4										
5122		4	3											2
103B (OP)		6		3	1									
102B (OP)	2	3	2											1
5225										2				
5233														
5223								4	3					
5221						4								
202A						3	2	3	2	1				
5325													2	
5333														
5323												4		
5321											4			
302A											3	3	1	
Jump	1	2	1	2		2	1	2	1		2	2		
3M														
5136					4									
5134				5										
5132		5												
5235										3				
5233								5						
5335													3	
5333												5		
5152														3
Jump		1		1		1		1			1	1		

Table 8.3   Platform Skills Progressions

GROUP I - FORWARD									
10M	101B(S)	103C(S)	103C	103B(S)	103B	105B	107C	107B	109C
7.5M									
107C							4		
105B						7			
103B					8				
103B(S)				8					
103C			9						
103C(S)		7							
101B(S)	8								
5M									
107C									3
105B								2	
105C							3		
103B					7	5			
103B(S)				7					
103C			8						
103C(S)		6							
101B(S)	7								
101B (S-OP)	6	5		6					
101B (OP)			7		6				
Line-up	5	4	6	5	5	6			
3M									
105C									2
103B						5			
103B(S)									
103C			5						
103C(S)		3							
102B					4	4			
102B(S)				4					
102C			4						
102C(S)		4							
101B(S)	4								
101B (S-OP)	3			3					
101B (OP)			3		3	3			
101C(S)		3							
1M									
103B								1	
103C							2		1
102B					2	2			
102C			2				1		
102B(S)				2					
102C(S)		2							
101B(S)	2								

(Cont.)

Table 8.3   (Continued)

GROUP I - FORWARD (Cont.)								
1M	101B(S)	103C(S)	103C	103B(S)	103B	105B	107C	107B	109C
101B (S-OP)	1			1					
101B (OP)					1	1			
101C(S)		1							
101C			1						

GROUP II - BACKWARD							
10M	201A	201B	203A	203B	205C	205B	207C
7.5M							
206C							4
205C					7		
203B				11			
203A			3				
201B		9					
201A	8						
Jump	7	8		10			
5M							
205C							3
204C					5		
204B						5	
203C					9		
203B				9		4	
202B				7			
202A			2				
201B		7					
201A	6						
Jump	4	6	1	6	3	3	
Line-up	5			8	6	6	
3M							
204C							2
203C							1
202B				4			
201B		5					
201C		4					
Jump	2	3		3			
Line-up	3	2		5			
1M							
202B				2		2	
202C					2		
Jump	1	1		1	1	1	

Table 8.3   (Continued)

GROUP III - REVERSE							
10M	301A	301B	303C	303B	305C	305B	307C
7.5M							
306C							5
305C					5		
303B				5			
303C			6				
301B		8					
301A	6						
Jump		7					
5M							
305C							4
304C					3		
304B						3	
303C			5		2		
303B						2	
302B				4			
302C			4				
301A	5						
301B		6					
301C					4		
Jump	4	5					
3M							
304C							3
303C							2
302B				3			
302C			3				
301B		4					
301C	3	3					
Jump	2	2	2	2			
1M							
302B						1	
302C					1		1
Jump	1	1	1	1			

(Cont.)

Table 8.3   (Continued)

GROUP IV - INWARD							
10M	401A	401B	403C	403B	405C	405B	407C
7.5M							
405C					5		
403B				4			
403C			6				
401B		6					
401A	5						
5M							
405C							3
403B				3		3	
403C			5		4		
401B		5					
401A	4						
401B (OP)	3	4	4			1	
3M							
403C					4		
403B						4	
402B				3		2	
402C			3				
401B		3					
401B (OP)	2			2			
401C		2	2		3		
1M							
403C							2
402C					2		
401B (OP)	1			1			
401C		1	1		1		1

Table 8.3   (Continued)

| | | | | | | | GROUP V - TWISTING | | | | | | | | |

10M	5132	5134	5136	5231	5233	5235	5237	5331	5333	5335	5337	5152 in	5152 out	5154 in	5154 out
7.5M															
5152												2	2		2
5333									3						
5331								3							
5235						6									
5233				4	3										
5231															
5136			4												
5134		6	3												
5132	5	4													
5M															
5327											3				
5325										3	2				
5323									2	2					
5331								2							
302A									1	1	1				
5227							3								
5225						5	2								
5223				3	4	4									
5231															
202A					3	3	1								
5134															1
5132	4	3										1			
103B (OP)	3	2													
3M															
5321								1							
5223					2	2									
5221				2											
202A				1	1	1									
5124		5	2												
5122	2														
102B (OP)	1	1	1												
103C-B															
1M															
103C-B													1		1

(Cont.)

Table 8.3   (Continued)

GROUP VI - ARMSTAND					
10M	631C	632C	634C	612C-B	614C-B	616C
7.5M						
614C-B					2	
612C-B				3		
632C		5				
631C	4					
5M						
614C						2
612C-B				2	1	
633C			3			
632C		4	2			
631C	3	2				
3M						
614C						3
612C-B					1	
611C-B				1		
631C	2	1				
1M						
631C	1	3	1			
612C						1

GLOSSARY

backward press—A press in which the diver springs from the board or platform while performing a takeoff standing backward.

backward save—An underwater motion in which the diver arches the body and bends the knees, drawing the heels toward the buttocks, to keep the legs entering the water vertically.

bottom of the press—The point in the forward and backward springing movements at which the diver fully flexes the legs and hips prior to extending the legs and jumping into the takeoff.

calling—Giving a verbal cue for the diver to come out of a dive.

checking—Using action–reaction movements or lengthening the body to slow somersault rotation.

circular closure—Method with which the diver accelerates backward and reverse somersaulting dives by moving the arms backward and downward from the takeoff position, to grasp the legs.

C position—The general body shape the diver assumes to initiate backward and reverse somersaulting dives.

direct closure—Method with which the diver accelerates backward and reverse somersaulting dives by bringing the arms to the legs in a direct line of movement.

drive leg—The leg used in the hurdle to push the diver from the springboard or platform.

dry-land springboard—A diving stand and springboard installed in an area away from the pool, with a foam rubber landing pit.

forward approach—In springboard or platform diving, an approach that consists of 3 or more steps plus a hurdle from one foot to a two-foot landing on the end of the board.

hollow position—A concave shape of the front side of the body.

hurdle—A jump from one foot to a two-foot takeoff from the end of the springboard or platform.

hurdle leg—The leg that is lifted into the air at the beginning of the hurdle.

one-piece movement—Technique in which the diver moves the upper body, head, and arms simultaneously in a piking action, to initiate forward and inward somersaulting dives.

opposition—The point in the backward press when the arms move upward and the heels move downward.

preliminary takeoff position—The position of the body when the springboard is at maximum depression.

press—The action of the diver depressing the springboard or, in platform diving, loading the body weight onto the legs prior to takeoff.

rip entry—An entry into the water that creates little splash and is accompanied by a sound similar to fabric ripping.

somersault save—An underwater somersaulting technique that aids the diver in controlling the angle of entry of the legs.

square-out—The method of stopping the twist in dives that combine somersaulting and twisting.

step length—The distance from the top of the fibula to the ground, plus the foot length. This represents the length of the step measured from the toes of the trailing leg to the toes of the lead leg, while the diver is performing a moderate speed of steps.

stuck—A diver's feeling that a somersaulting dive is not rotating very fast.

swimming the entry—A breaststrokelike movement of the arms used immediately after entry impact that aids the rip entry technique.

takeoff—Series of movements that take place from the beginning of the springing motion on the end of the springboard or platform, until the feet leave the takeoff area.

top of the press—The point during the backward press technique when the diver is standing high on the toes, with the body straight and arms overhead, in preparation for dropping the body weight into the springboard or platform.

visual spotting—The technique with which the diver visually sees specific areas to aid in orientation in somersaulting dives.

INDEX

Prices subject to change.

8/99